RETRIEVER
TRAINING TESTS

James B. Spencer

ARCO PUBLISHING, INC.
NEW YORK

Published by Arco Publishing, Inc.
215 Park Avenue South, New York, N.Y. 10003

Library of Congress Cataloging in Publication Data

Spencer, James B.
   Retriever training tests.

   Includes index.
   1. Retrievers.   2. Dogs—Training.   I. Title.
SF429.R4S63   1983   636.7'52   83-3709
ISBN 0-668-05681-9

Printed in the United States of America

10   9   8   7   6   5   4   3   2   1

DEDICATION

My youngest son, Pat, started throwing birds for me and my training groups before he was big enough to throw very far. In fact, we started him out with a Retrieve-R-Trainer, which propels a dummy with .22-caliber blank shells. For years he went out to assist me with my dogs every evening—spring, summer, and early fall. He put up with heat, cold, mosquitoes, chiggers, and my own sometimes bad disposition, and he seldom complained. As I look at the diagrams for the various tests in this book, I realize that Pat has been the "gun" and the blind planter at every position in every test—many times. As a small token of my appreciation for his generous assistance, I dedicate this book to him. Without him it would never have been conceived.

CONTENTS

PREFACE

My three-month-old golden retriever, Belle (Belvedere Rumrunner Gin), and I had a good session this evening. I started her introduction into water a little later than I usually do; as a matter of fact, this was only her third time "at sea." Tonight I found a spot on the Big Ditch near Wichita, Kansas, that was perfect for what I wanted to do with Belle. It was a quiet pool some 25 yards across and about thigh-deep for me. There I was able to wade across and encourage Belle to swim along behind me. I did, and she did, and all went beautifully. Oh, she beat the water a little with her front feet, but time will cure that. The important thing is that she did not hesitate to jump in and swim after me.

As I happily put Belle into her kennel run afterward, I noticed that my nine-year-old golden, Brandy (Rumrunner's Brandy***), is somewhat fat and out of shape. He has been semiretired for some time now ("semiretired" means that he no longer competes in field trials, but he still hunts with my two sons and me every fall). I will have to get him back in shape soon, for the hunting season is not far off. Getting him in shape is a happy prospect. I have said many times that if I were out training my dogs and someone convinced me that the world would end the next day, I would not be able to worry about that until the training session was over. I might panic then, but not before. That is what a hobby should do for us: it should so absorb our attention that nothing else can get through for as long as we are involved with our hobby.

As I entered the house, I was greeted by my golden, Duffy (Duncan Dell's MacDuff** CD), now fourteen and a half years

---

*** A triple asterisk after a dog's name indicates that he is a "Qualified All-Age Dog." This means that he has placed first or second in the qualifying stake or satisfactorily completed the amateur or open stake in a licensed field trial.

** A double asterisk after a dog's name indicates that he has competed successfully in a licensed field trial, but is not a qualified all-age dog.

old. Duffy is the equivalent of a one-hundred-year-old man—and he moves like one, to tell the truth. Duffy has been with the Spencer clan since he was seven weeks old. I have often described him as a three-sport letterman, because he has placed in several licensed field trials, won a CD title in obedience trials, and earned several bench championship points at dog shows. He is much more than that, however. He helped raise the five Spencer kids, allowed them to drag him around the ring in junior showmanship competition, retrieved the first birds that each of our two boys shot, shared duck blinds, boats, and sometimes the back seat of the car with us. He has sat patiently and watched me miss duck after duck after duck on "those days"—and I have more of them than most hunters do. Duffy has put up with my training errors and survived them when many dogs would have crumpled. Since his full retirement, he has been a house dog, and he loves that life almost as much as he used to love competing in field trials and hunting. (I think he loved field trials more than hunting because he got to retrieve more birds per day in trials than he usually did while hunting.) Duffy is a member of the Spencer family.

Duffy won't be with us much longer. We know it, and we exchange anxious glances when he slips and falls in the kitchen or has trouble with the two steps that lead into the house from the back yard. He is almost completely deaf, but he knows us so well that his hearing problem is not apparent to people who visit us. Maybe he reads our lips, or maybe he just knows by our physical attitudes what we are saying to him—as long as he is looking at us. When he isn't looking, we can tell that he doesn't hear much nowadays.

It won't be long for Duffy. He has had a good life for a retriever, however, and the Spencer clan has had a better life as a family because of him.

When and where did this involvement with retrievers start for me? I have thought about that and can find no simple answer.

Some of my most pleasant early memories are of my Grandfather Kirkpatrick. On warm summer evenings he used to sit in a lawn chair in the front yard of his Council Bluffs, Iowa, home and tell me stories about hunting and fishing. He had done a little market hunting around the turn of the century. He made his own decoys, and he could call ducks without an instrument. He died in 1939 when I was only twelve, before I had the chance to go hunting with him. Still, I am sure that it was he who planted a love of duck hunting in my young mind, and my interest in dogs came after that.

In 1947 I hunted with a retriever for the first time. Paul

DeKlots, a friend of my father and my Uncle Fred, had a female golden retriever named Ginger. Paul, Dad, and Uncle Fred took me along on pheasant and duck hunting trips back then, and I marveled at what that dog could do. Looking back now, I can see that Ginger was a very ordinary retriever, and not too well trained. Still, she brought our birds back to us. Wow, what a dog, I thought. Sometimes now, when I have a frustrating session trying to train one of my dogs in really advanced work, I look at my dog as I did Ginger back in 1947. I look at what he can do rather than what he is failing to do, and it gives me a fresh outlook—for a few moments at least. Ginger probably started my interest in retrievers.

In 1958 a man named Sim Bowles came to my door with a five-month-old golden retriever on lead. He told me that he and his wife had talked to me at a recent obedience trial—I was then training a female weimaraner for obedience trials and hunting—and that when they asked me what breed they should get, I told them that a golden would be perfect for them. I didn't remember the conversation, but I was given to rashness in my youth, so I never doubted it. Sim asked me if I would help him train his golden for field trials and hunting. I told him I knew nothing about such training, that I was a pointing dog man, and so on. He reminded me that I had recommended the breed to him, and he told me that he had never hunted in his life, much less trained a dog, and he really needed help. What could I say? We found a copy of James Lamb Free's classic, *Training Your Retriever,* and we trained Sim's golden, Rocco, chapter by chapter. The dog was so good that the training worked just as the book promised. The only other time I have had such a pleasant surprise was the day I first tried calling ducks, with only an instruction manual to guide me. The ducks came tumbling in just as if Grandpa Kirkpatrick were calling them for me. Sim Bowles and Rocco started me in training retrievers.

In 1968, after a period of competing in field trials with German shorthaired pointers and another period of playing golf—a game for which I am unusually ill-suited—I bought my first golden, Duffy. I was fortunate enough to get a dog that traced back to Sim Bowles's breeding. Sim was dead by that time, but the Duncan Dell kennel name that he started was still being used, and I sought that prefix because of Sim.

Since then I have been deeply involved in retrievers, retriever training, and field trials, as well as in hunting, of course. There have been many retrievers: Duffy, Brandy, Mickey, Pirate, Tina, BB, and Pepper (a Labrador). I have started my own kennel name, Rumrunner, and have conducted training classes for those who have purchased Rumrunner puppies. I have also conducted training classes for the Jayhawk Retriever Club, and in these I worked with Labradors more than with goldens.

I have spent a good deal of time teaching beginners how to train their dogs. Next to training dogs myself, I enjoy working with beginners more than any other part of my involvement with dogs. The teacher usually learns more than the students and gets to meet some very nice people. Working with beginners has kept me from growing stale or becoming too set in any one way of training.

During my days with retrievers many, besides my dogs and my students, have taught me. There is no such thing as an untaught teacher, at least among human beings.

Professional trainer Jim Robinson had the nearly impossible task of trying to get me to listen to him when I took Duffy to him for help with a suction problem I had created when Duffy was first learning blind retrieves. Jim worked with Duffy and me for about eight months. He worked wonders with Duffy, but I am sure that he felt all along that he was wasting his time with me, that I was not accepting what he said. That wasn't the case; I just had to let all the information incubate in my hard head and let it get translated into my vernacular, so to speak. I still remember most of what Jim told me, and I have come to accept almost all of it. If I stay in this game long enough, I may buy everything he said. He has since moved to another part of the country, where he will never know the satisfaction of seeing that I follow so much of what he tried to teach me years ago. Jim once characterized me as "half golden and half Chesapeake," and I must admit that he was right.

Darrell Kincaid, one of the best field trial judges in the nation, has taught me much about test design, whether he knows it or not. I have always respected him as a judge, so I have studied the tests he has set up at trials I have attended, even when I have not been entered in the stake he judged. Darrell is a merry Scot and a real gentleman.

Pro Jane Laman, a retired teacher who once specialized in handling very difficult students, has been a great influence on me. Even though I have never trained with her, we have often talked at both fun trials and licensed trials.

When I have encountered a serious training problem that I couldn't solve, I have gone to La Cygne, Kansas, and talked to D. L. Walters and his wife Ann. They kept Brandy at their place for three months when he was having a popping problem, and they worked wonders with him. There are times when you are better off taking your dog to a pro than wasting your time and ruining the dog with your own methods—which obviously aren't working too well, for if they were, you wouldn't have a problem. In this book, I will point out the problems that you should refer to a pro. Look at it this way: you brush your own teeth, but when you have a cavity, you go to a dentist. Use the services of the professional dog trainer in the same way.

Many others have contributed to this book. No book has a single author. There is usually a body of knowledge understood and shared by many, and then one day someone says, "Hey, this should be written down for others." That person writes the book and is said to be the author, but he is more often merely the one who beats on the typewriter, not the originator of all the information.

A book is a gift from many to many.

INTRODUCTION

Every year thousands of people acquire their first retrievers: Labrador, golden, Chesapeake Bay, flat-coated, curly-coated, Irish water spaniel, or American water spaniel. Most of these people intend to train their new dogs for some kind of field work. Although many beginners are interested only in hunting at first, some of them develop an interest in field trials after they have been exposed to them—and they surely will be within a year or so. A growing number of new trainers also develop an interest in the working certificate tests offered by the various national breed clubs such as the Labrador Retriever Club of America, the Golden Retriever Club of America, and the American Chesapeake Club. These working certificate tests were designed primarily to determine whether dogs that do not compete in field trials, especially bench show dogs (those bred for and exhibited in conformation shows), have good basic retrieving instincts. Some of the tests have been expanded and are challenging enough to require fairly serious training. The WCX (Working Certificate Excellent) offered by the Golden Retriever Club of America is a good example. To earn the WCX, a dog must do a triple marked retrieve on land and a double marked retrieve in water. Those are not trivial accomplishments.

Every year thousands of new retriever owners start out to train their dogs for one or more of these: hunting, field trials, or working certificates. They start out with high enthusiasm, a stack of training books, and a spouse and/or children as assistants (every retriever trainer needs assistants to throw birds, plant blind retrieves, and so forth). Unfortunately, very few owners are still training a year later. Most give up and go back to golf or bowling.

This annual crop of new retriever trainers can be compared with the biblical parable of the sower and the seed: some seed fell on rocky soil and never took root (the trainers who start with dogs that cannot be trained); some seed fell among thorns and after sprouting were choked out (the trainers who start with good dogs

xiii

but who ruin them through ignorance—probably the largest group); and some seed fell on good ground and brought forth fruit manyfold (the few who succeed).

Those who start with basically untrainable dogs can be helped only by being convinced that they need new dogs. All too often, however, these owners feel that the fault is theirs, not their dogs'. Professional retriever trainers are sometimes asked to train dogs that aren't worth the time and effort. They recognize the problem right away and drop these dogs in favor of others that can be trained. Beginners don't recognize the problem, so they continue with their untrainable animals until they become convinced that retriever training is beyond their capabilities. This is unfortunate.

How do you know if your retriever is not worth training? If the dog shows little interest in retrieving after you have worked for a couple of months, assuming the dog is six to eight months old, you should probably take the retriever to a competent professional trainer for an evaluation. This won't cost much, and it could save you months of frustrating effort.

Those who start with good dogs but who get mired in their training program after good initial results probably constitute the largest part of the annual crop of new owners. Things go very well for the beginners at first, and then their dogs seem to get worse instead of better every day. The dogs fail every training test until eventually they lose all interest in retrieving.

The problem here usually is the owners' ignorance of the environmental factors in retriever training. These trainers typically buy several training manuals and read them religiously. From the books they acquire a good deal of insight into the dog–human relationship in retriever training but next to nothing about how to set up training tests and nothing at all about what makes a test easy or hard for the dog. To make matters worse, they frequently go to field trials and see what kinds of tests are used there. Field trials, however, are meant to challenge the best professionally trained dogs in the country; pros take their strings of dogs all over the nation to compete. The tests in such trials are very difficult, far beyond the capabilities of the novice puppy and owner. Beginning trainers do not realize this, so they think that they are doing the right thing by simulating field trial tests in their training sessions.

New trainers also let their imaginations run wild in designing tests of their own. Seldom are they satisfied with the basics; only the bizarre interests them. In the training classes I conduct for new owners of puppies from my own Rumrunner line of golden retrievers, and for the Jayhawk Retriever Club, I spend al-

Figure 1.   A black Labrador brings in a drake mallard.

most as much time trying to teach people how to set up good, solid tests as anything else. After a few sessions, I have the owners start setting up tests for their own dogs. These sessions are a revelation. Before I allow any dog to run the test, I ask the test designer why he or she set it up this way. Typically, the owner has no answer, or a very vague one. Then I ask what the handler hopes to teach the dog with this particular arrangement. Again, I get no answer. Finally, I ask what the difficulties are with this test. No answer. It then becomes necessary for me to explain the test so that the designer understands what he or she is asking the dogs to do. If the exercise is within the dogs' capabilities, I let them run the test. If not, I help the new trainer change it to something more suitable. Quite a few sessions are necessary before most people learn to set up reasonable tests for their dogs.

Most new trainers become too absorbed in the dog–human relationship and too unconcerned about the environmental factors involved in training. These environmental factors include wind, terrain, cover, placement and sequence of the falls, and artificial factors such as decoys. A slight change in any one of these factors can change a very easy test into an extremely difficult one. New trainers need to understand this, but there is no way they can acquire this insight unless they have the opportunity to work with an experienced trainer.

This book is intended for such new trainers; it will describe and explain the environmental factors involved in setting up good solid tests.

In addition to reading about training, you can get expert help from a professional trainer or from a good amateur. Going to a good professional is probably the best way to train your dog. By this I mean having the pro teach you how to train your own dog. Most professional trainers offer this service, although they may prefer to train the dog themselves because they earn more money that way and the work is easier. Dogs are easier to train than new dog trainers. Ask any pro.

The assistance of a good amateur doesn't compare with that of a pro, but it is better than stumbling along on your own. Some retriever clubs offer training classes to new members. If the instructors are knowledgeable and sincerely interested in helping the students, such a class can be an excellent resource.

Figure 2.   A golden retriever hits the water.

With these approaches, however, you could end up with a well-trained dog and still not understand the training process. Experienced trainers, both professional and amateur, are usually better at setting up tests than they are at explaining them. You could train a dog this way and not be much better off than you were initially when it is time to train your next dog. Ask many questions when you are working with a pro or an experienced amateur.

What This Book Is

This book contains a collection of diagrams of training tests, each with an explanation of the significant environmental factors: wind, terrain, cover, and placement and sequence of falls. It is not an exhaustive collection of tests—that would be impossible, for new tests are being designed all the time—but the collection is sufficient to allow beginners to understand the significant elements of test structure. The book will enable novices to understand the subtleties of tests that they encounter at field trials, in working certificate tests, and in hunting.

Each chapter of this book explains a different type of test: single marked retrieve, double marked retrieve, triple marked retrieve, basic blind retrieve, and suction blind retrieve. Each chapter builds on the work in the previous chapters.

Single marked retrieves are tests in which only one bird is thrown and the dog is allowed to see it thrown. The retriever sees all birds that are thrown in marked retrieves or, more simply, marks. The dog does not see the bird thrown in blind retrieves, however.

Double marked retrieves, or doubles, are tests in which two birds are thrown in different places and the dog has to remember both of them and retrieve them one at a time. Dogs will first retrieve the second bird thrown and then will retrieve the first bird thrown. For this reason, the first bird thrown is called the memory bird and the second one thrown is called the diversion.

Triple marked retrieves, or triples, are like doubles except that three birds are thrown in three different places. The dog has to remember all three and retrieve them one at a time.

All marking tests require a "gun" for each bird. The gun is a person who throws the bird and fires a .22-caliber blank shell. In these tests we use dead birds or dummies. When live birds, ("fliers") are used, three people are needed: one to throw the bird and two to shoot it.

Figure 3.   A Chesapeake Bay retriever waits by the blind.

Basic blind retrieves are those tests in which a dog doesn't see a bird thrown but is handled to it by whistle and arm signals. Basic blinds include no artificial diversions to draw the dog away from the bird—no marked retrieves, no other blind retrieves in the same test, no dry guns, and so forth. Only wind, terrain, and cover conditions are used to make the test more difficult.

Suction blind retrieves are those in which artificial factors are used to make the test more difficult. Examples of such factors are blinds, marks, dry guns, scented areas, and decoys.

Each chapter contains training tests illustrating the environmental factors that can affect a dog's performance. In addition, part of each chapter is devoted to training tips and handling techniques. The training tips are not intended to constitute a complete training program, but they do cover certain training problems that have not been adequately covered elsewhere in retriever training literature. They also cover a few approaches that—while certainly not new and not invented by me—have not been well documented before. The handling techniques are divided into hunting and field trial situations, and they are intended to help you make your dog's job easier by the manner in which you handle the various retrieving problems. Even the casual observer at a retriever field trial can spot the green handlers and can recognize the mistakes that often cause the dogs to fail the tests.

So little has been written about proper handling techniques that a new owner needs years of trial and error to develop methods of handling that help rather than hinder the dog. Hunting is more difficult than trial work because in a duck blind there are no good handlers to watch and imitate. A duck blind usually accommodates only one dog and one handler, so beginners can hunt for years and never discover their mistakes. The handling suggestions in this book will offer some insight and assistance to beginning handlers.

The training test diagrams and explanations, however, are the heart of this book. Ignorance of the environmental factors the dog has to deal with in every retrieve causes the most harm in every handler–retriever relationship—and the ignorance is on the part of the handler, not the dog.

What This Book Is Not

This book is not a training manual per se. It does not offer a complete training program, although it is full of suggestions for training a dog to cope with various environmental factors. Furthermore, this is not intended to be your one and only training book. Several excellent books are available, all of which provide good, overall training programs. You should read them and reread them as you progress with your retriever. They tell you how to introduce your dog to single, double, triple, and blind retrieves. They also tell you how to start your dog in water, how to force-break a retriever, and how to do many other things not dealt with in this book. Those books deal extensively with the handler–dog relationship in training whereas this book deals principally with the dog–environment relationship and what the trainer needs to know about it.

This book does not advise you about which retriever breed to choose. That choice is a personal one. I am blessed (or cursed) with a high regard for the golden retriever. It's true that I get tired of pulling burrs out of their long, luxuriant coats. It's also true that they do not dominate the action at field trials (Labs do). Goldens are not even a native American breed, as is the Chesapeake. Nevertheless, I love them, and I am willing to put up with their drawbacks to get their more desirable traits: trainability, gentleness, beauty, and good nose. Others feel the same way about the other breeds. Each has advantages and disadvantages. You have to decide what you really want in a dog, what good points you are willing to live without, and what bad points you think you can put up with.

This book does not tell you how to select a good puppy. That subject is dealt with definitively in *Training Your Retriever,* the classic by James Lamb Free. There is nothing I can say to make Free's message any clearer.

This book does not tell you how to raise and feed your puppy or how to breed good retrievers. There are many other books on these subjects.

How to Use This Book

You should probably read this book once quickly to get the overall picture. Then consult the individual chapters in your day-to-day training program. The chapters are arranged progressively, from the simplest tests to the most difficult, so the book should parallel your own program quite closely.

You should not limit yourself to the exact tests diagrammed here. You might start out using them just as they are drawn, but it is important for you to learn the elements that make up these tests so you can design tests of your own. You should not memorize the tests and use them by rote. On the contrary, the tests and your dog's response to them should be an educational experience for you. These tests should be your introduction to an understanding of the environmental factors involved in test design. You will never learn everything, of course, but neither will anyone else.

If you are to be successful, either you need to gain an understanding of the basics of test design or you must work with someone who has such an understanding—or you can do both. Whichever method you choose, this book can help you if you use it thoughtfully.

If you have field trial aspirations for your dog, you will use every chapter in this book before you are through. If you are interested only in the working certificate tests, you will not need to use the chapters on blind retrieves—at least not yet. Eventually, blind retrieves will probably be put into the working certificate programs, but that hasn't happened yet. If you are interested in training for hunting only, you will have to decide how much of the book you should use. Do you want your dog to do triples and blind retrieves, or will singles and doubles be enough?

If my dogs could not do blind retrieves, I would lose a lot of ducks and a few pheasants. Your experience may be different, however. Perhaps your dog has a knack for looking at the exact duck that you are shooting at in every flock. Mine doesn't. Maybe your dog doesn't go behind the blind and take a nap when things get slow. Mine does. Sometimes a single duck slips into sight at that time, and I wake up just in time to nick it lightly (I'm not the greatest shot on the marsh) and it glides some 200 yards before it comes down—all before my dog moves around to the front of the blind where he can see. Maybe your dog isn't so often on the other side of a dense hedge when a rooster pheasant explodes right in front of you. Mine is. The bird frequently struggles to the other side of a big pond and then folds before my dog manages to get through the hedge. As you can see, my dogs have to be able to do blind retrieves if they are going to pick up a reasonable share of the birds I hit. Besides, I enjoy blind retrieve training for the sense of teamwork it gives.

Regardless of what you are training your retriever for, use the structure of field trial training. It is well organized and well documented, and it will succeed with any dog worth training. Dogs trained for field trials will be able to handle 90 percent of the hunting situations they encounter. Actually, the only training I give my own dogs specifically for hunting is an introduction to getting into and out of a boat and the command "Hunt 'em out," for searching for a bird known to have fallen in a specific area.

This training is highly useful, and I learned about it from Dave Duffy's wonderful book, *Hunting Dog Know-How*. Other than that, my dogs hunt with nothing more than their field trial training. Yours will, too.

Try to form a training group of three to six people, each with no more than one or two dogs. If you can, find someone with trial experience. If not, you and your beginning friends can take turns setting up tests. Be sure that all of you know what you are trying to accomplish with each test. Have specific goals for each training session, and design your tests to help you attain those goals. Each of you should explain your own tests. After your dogs begin to look good in training, try to find a retriever club that sponsors fun trials, which are informal field trials for local dogs. The tests are usually much simpler than those used in licensed trials. Watch a fun trial or two, and then, if you think your dog can handle the tests you see, enter one and find out. Fun trials are good experi-

Figure 4.   A yellow Labrador chases down a crippled mallard.

ence for you and your dog, and they are neither as expensive nor as highly competitive as licensed trials.

When you and your dog are ready for licensed trials, you will know it; you won't have to ask. Many people compete in fun trials with their hunting dogs all spring, summer, and early fall and never think of entering a licensed trial. There is no better way to keep a good hunting dog sharp, and you will meet a number of people who share your interest in the sport. You might even find some new places to hunt.

Can This Book Help Owners of Other Breeds?

All sporting breeds are expected to retrieve: the continental (or bobtailed) pointing breeds, the spaniels, and to a lesser degree the other pointers and the setters. None of them can be expected to do the advanced work required of the true retriever breeds, however. They lack the physical qualities, the instincts, and the temperament required for the work expected of retrievers. Still, they are often called on to retrieve in a limited way. They are subject to the same environmental influences in their retrieving as are the true retriever breeds. Because these influences are covered in this book, it will be useful to trainers of these other breeds, too.

Whenever I point out the differences in the level of work expected of a retriever and that asked of one of the other sporting breeds, I remember a three-legged German shorthaired pointer that was brought out to a fun trial held by the Jayhawk Retriever Club many years ago. In fun trials at that time, we held what we called the hunters' stake. It was for retrievers who were just good old meat dogs, with little training or ability. Therefore, the tests were restricted to single marked retrieves. It was a popular stake with some of the members. It sometimes took five or six different tests to find a winner, which meant that the entrants got plenty of work whether they won anything or not.

We used to allow people to enter breeds other than retrievers in the hunters' stake. Many tried to win with Brittanies, springers, and Irish setters, but none of them ever placed.

Then one day a man entered his three-legged German shorthaired pointer. One of the dog's back legs had been amputated because of an injury, and he was over eight years old. I thought that the owner was out of his mind when he entered this dog.

There were about fifteen dogs entered—fourteen Labradors and the one German shorthair. With all his other problems, he also had the numerical odds against him. The Labs were not first- or even second-rate dogs, but they had all been bred specifically to retrieve—and each of them had four legs. None was over three years old.

It was a hot summer day, and the heat sapped the energy from the dogs as they took their turns at one single mark after another. The three-legged shorthair seemed to suffer the most since it took him so much longer to hobble the 60 to 80 yards to the fall. Once he got there, however, he didn't waste any time. He just picked up the bird and hobbled back. Most of the Labs were having trouble finding the birds after they reached the area, but not the old shorthair.

The gallery watched intently as the old shorthair picked up bird after bird with no problem. We felt sorry for the old fellow as he hobbled all over the pasture in the extreme heat. We were so concerned about his age and his handicap that it was well into the stake before we realized that this three-legged shorthair was winning—and by a wide margin. Never before had a dog of any nonretriever breed placed, and here was this shorthaired pointer showing our Labs how the work should be done! He won it going away.

That dog taught me what some of the nonretrieving breeds can do. Yes, their trainers can get something out of this book.

About the Diagrams

The diagrams in this book are fairly easy to understand, especially for anyone familiar with basic retriever training procedures. For those as yet unfamiliar with them, I will offer a brief explanation.

The "line" is the starting point for the dog and handler. The handler takes the dog to the line, and the dog sits there at heel until the birds are thrown (in all marking tests).

Each bird is indicated on the diagrams by an X. In the chapters on marking tests, all X's are marked falls. In the chapter on basic blind retrieves, all X's are birds planted for blind retrieves. In the chapter on suction blinds, each X is identified as either a blind or a marked retrieve.

The "guns"—actually the bird throwers in marking tests—

are indicated on the diagrams by small black circles. A dotted line indicates where the gun throws the mark.

Land and water are appropriately marked wherever the difference is significant.

In the multiple marking tests, the numbers indicate the throwing sequence. The number 1 indicates the first bird thrown; 2 the second; 3 the third.

No lengths are marked on the diagrams. Distances can vary, depending on the stage of training of the dog, the purposes for which the dog is being trained, the terrain, the cover, and so forth. Considerations of length are discussed in the introductory remarks to each chapter.

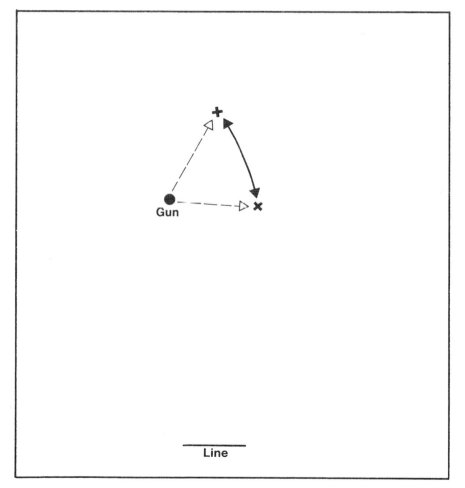

Figure 5.   Possible angle of throw.

All the marks in the diagrams are drawn at approximately the same angle to the line. In practice, however, the angle of the throw can vary from slightly in—toward the line, but only slightly—to sharply away from the line. In setting up tests for training, you should use all reasonable angles so the dog doesn't expect the bird to be in a certain spot in relation to the guns every time. It is not reasonable to throw the bird right at or directly away from the dog, but any angle between "slightly in" and "sharply back" is all right. "Slightly in" means that the angle from the line to the guns and then to the bird is about 80 degrees. "Sharply back" means that the angle does not exceed 150 degrees. These are about the extremes that you will see in field trials.

The length of the throw—how far the guns actually propel the dummy or the bird—is also a consideration. If ducks or pheasants are used, the guns should throw them as far as they can (it won't be too far). If small plastic dummies are used, the guns should be careful not to throw them more than 15 or 20 yards out. That is about as far as a duck or pheasant can be tossed, and that is what you are simulating with the dummies.

The height of the throw should be somewhat greater than the length. It is important to get the bird up where the dog can see it. If someone throws a "rabbit"—a bird that skims the ground—it should be picked up and thrown again. In fact, all badly thrown birds should be picked up and thrown again. A bad throw is called a "no bird" in field trials. There the judges decide when a throw is bad enough to be called a "no bird." In training, it is up to the handler to decide. Make sure your dog gets decent throws in training. Don't hesitate to call a "no bird" if you think that one of the throws was not good enough.

1. SINGLE MARKED RETRIEVES

Training Tips

A single marked retrieve is a test in which only one bird is thrown for the dog to retrieve and the dog is allowed to watch it fall. In fact, the dog watches the birds fall in all marked tests, which are intended to determine how well the dog "marks" the birds. Tests in which the dog doesn't see the birds thrown are called blind retrieves. These are treated in later chapters.

A single marked retrieve—or a single mark, as it is more often called—can occur on land or in water, and each element presents its own problems for the dog. Water is the more difficult environment, no matter how much the dog enjoys it. Dogs move more slowly in water, so they have to remember where a bird fell longer there than they do on land.

In hunting, the single mark is probably the one that dogs see most often. Perhaps 70 percent of their work is on single marks, even in the duck blind, where multiple marks are to be expected.

In field trials the single mark is rare except in puppy stakes at fun trials. There is an occasional single mark in the derby stake, even in licensed trials, and you will see a single mark mixed with one or two blind retrieves in the all-age stakes from time to time, but the single marked retrieve is not a major exercise in field trials.

Nevertheless, the single mark is the first type of test every retriever is trained on, whether the dog is a hunter or a field trial prospect.

It is a good idea to start on bare ground with big white plastic dummies and to start with very short throws. Lengthen the throws as rapidly as your dog will allow. Some retrievers have no

1

problem with length on bare ground; others do, at first anyway. One good way to train for longer throws is to have the dog make the same retrieve several times, each time from farther away. The thrower stays in the same place and makes the same throw each time, but the handler runs back away from the line while the dog is going after the dummy. That way the dog starts for the retrieve from a little farther away from the mark each time. The dog never sees the handler move because the handler runs away while the dog is going after the dummy. When the dog turns around to return, the handler is standing still—but ten or fifteen yards farther away from the dog than before. Most dogs take to this technique very well; they hardly notice that each retrieve is longer. Since each dummy is thrown to the same place, the little extra distance between the dog and the fall each time is not a problem.

The same technique can be used in cover after the dog has finished the bare-ground work. Using this method, a trainer can easily lengthen a dog's retrieving ability from about 20 yards to 50 or 60 on a given test in one training session without risking failure. The dog knows exactly where the bird is each time and simply has to run a little farther to get to that place.

I like to have a dog steady, or reasonably so, when I start serious work in cover. Dogs that are steady—that sit at your side at the line after the dummy is thrown until ordered to retrieve— mark better than dogs that break and run full-tilt as the dummy goes up and comes down. It is a good idea to do your steadying on bare ground using big white dummies so there is no danger of the dog not finding the bird after being corrected for breaking. It doesn't take long to steady a retriever if you do it early enough, before the dog forms a bad habit of breaking.

Work in water should lag somewhat behind land work. This is true of all retriever training, for a couple of reasons. First, the dog should be self-confident in a given type of test before being asked to do the same test in water. Second, getting to, helping, or correcting a dog is much more difficult in the water. You should have most corrections out of the way when you put your dog in water on a new test.

If you are training a puppy, you must be sure that the dog is comfortable in water and able to swim without panic before you ask for a retrieve. To start a puppy in water, you should put on some old slacks and sneakers, wade in, and encourage the dog to follow you. Don't wear waders, for they will keep you from feeling water that is too cold for your dog. Later on, your dog may have to break skim ice to fetch a duck for you, but you don't want to start

Figure 6. Introducing a puppy to water. The trainer is not wearing waders. He is dressed in jeans so that he can be sure the water is warm enough. Notice that the puppy is beating the water with her front feet. This problem will correct itself with more experience.

out in water that is at all cold. Let the retriever learn to enjoy swimming first; adapting to cold water later will be no problem. Both Brandy and Duffy go with me to put out and pick up the decoys no matter how cold it is—and they could stay on shore and watch if they wanted to. Cold water just isn't a problem to them. Had I started them out in cold water, however, they might still be afraid of the wet stuff today.

Wading across a narrow creek is a good way to start a pup swimming. The dog has to go through the water to come to you, and the distance across is short, so there is very little fear involved. Be generous with your praise while your dog is coming to you and after he reaches you.

Work often—daily if possible—until the dog is comfortable in the water. Don't attempt any retrieves in water until you are sure that your dog is no longer afraid, and even then make the retrieves very short for some time. If you try to stretch out the length too fast, the dog may refuse to go at all, and then what will you do? It is better to go very slowly and have your dog cooperate.

For a long time, keep the marks in water highly visible. Use big white dummies and throw them into open water areas where

Figure 7.   Starting a puppy in retrieving. Notice that the trainer has not taken the dummy from the pup, but is petting her first. This encourages a good return.

your dog will be able to see them as they fall and after they hit the water. If you toss them into cover too soon, your dog may give up, turn around, and come back to you before swimming halfway to the dummy. Here again, you will ask yourself, "Now what do I do?" and you will get no good answer. Keep water marks in open water until your dog is quite far along in cover work on land—until the dog has learned to hunt the area of the fall intently and perseveringly.

Many dogs, as they come out of the water after a retrieve, will drop the dummy and shake the water out of their coats. Some will clamp their teeth down on the dummy and shake. Neither response is good, but both are quite natural. There are two ways of preventing this with the young puppy or any dog that has not yet been force-broken. First, you can try running away from the dog as soon as his feet hit bottom near shore. Most dogs will chase you. When your dog catches up to you, squat down and pet him for a while, take the dummy, and let the dog shake. If this doesn't work, meet him at the water's edge and take the dummy before he has a chance to come out and shake.

If your dog is somewhat possessive of the dummy, you should not try to take it away too quickly, or the dog will be reluctant to return to you at all. It is a good idea to spend a minute or two petting this type of dog before you even touch the dummy, whether you use the running-away technique or meet your retriever at the shore. Such a dog is less likely to drop the dummy than to clamp down and shake if you don't take steps to prevent it. When you get your hands on the dog, force him into a sitting position and hold him there so he cannot shake while you pet him.

This is not a complete training course for the single mark, but it does touch on a few points not well covered in retriever training literature.

Handling Techniques

HUNTING SITUATIONS

In hunting ducks over decoys from a blind, only two handling problems occur: positioning the dog so that he will be able to see the birds that fall, and being sure that he stays in position until it is time to retrieve.

Usually it is better to position the dog alongside the blind, preferably on the side opposite that from which you expect ducks to approach. There, the retriever's movements will not draw the attention of incoming birds to the area of the blind. Normally, ducks are not spooked by the presence of a dog, but if their attention is focused on the land around the blind, they might see something—a shiny shell casing, a sandwich wrapper, a glint from someone's glasses—that would cause them to spook. If the dog is positioned on the other side of the blind, however, the ducks will not see him at all, and he should still be able to mark the falls easily.

The dog should remain in position until sent to retrieve. This makes marking *all* the falls easier and ensures the dog's safety.

Sometimes several birds will be shot from a single flock, and the only way a dog can mark them all is to stay put until the birds are all down. A dog that is hot after the first bird hit will never see the others—or will not mark them very well. Dogs don't mark accurately when they are running or swimming.

Many years ago, when Duffy was a youngster, I took him duck hunting on a small pond I had leased. Since I was using a pit blind, I positioned Duffy behind it. He could see as well from there as from anywhere, and he was visible to the ducks no matter which side I put him on. It turned out to be a very slow day, so slow in fact that I fell asleep. I don't know how long a nap I took, but when I woke up, I saw two green-winged teal buzzing the decoys. Groggily, I grabbed my gun, stood up, and fired three times—all misses, I must confess. I did not realize that, while I was asleep, Duffy had come around to the front of the blind and gone to sleep. The gun muzzle wasn't a foot from his ears when it went off three times: *bang! bang! bang!* There may be a better way of making a young dog gun-shy, but I don't know what it is. Granted, Duffy had been gun-proofed in the traditional ways long before this incident, but it still took about a year of patient effort to bring him out of the shock of this one unfortunate experience.

I was lucky that I was able to salvage him. You can avoid this kind of trouble by seeing to it that your dog stays where you put him until you send him to retrieve. If this requires that you tether him or tie him to the blind somehow, then so be it. Nothing good can happen to a dog that is wandering around a duck blind. The hunter will be concentrating on incoming ducks, not on the dog. Naturally, you cannot keep your dog in one place all day. He needs to relieve himself now and then. Normally he can do this after a retrieve, but on a slow day you will have to let him loose once in a while.

In jump shooting ducks on foot—stalking along a stream or slew—it is important to keep your dog at heel until you have shot

the birds. If the dog will not heel without continuous verbal encouragement, you will never get close enough to the ducks to get a
shot.

Dove hunting around a pond is similar to decoyed duck
shooting, but walk-up dove shooting offers the dog owner a different problem, and a serious one. Doves are hunted during the early
part of the season, when the weather is still quite warm. Dogs can
become overheated very quickly then, and they can die from heat
prostration in a very short time. I know one man who lost a fine
field trial retriever this way, and I almost lost Duffy to the heat
once while we were walking up doves. Fortunately I was near the
Arkansas River, so when Duffy started acting woozy, I was able to
carry him to the water and submerge him in it. He lay there in the
shallow water without moving for fully fifteen minutes and then
spent another quiet fifteen minutes before he was ready to stand
up. He wanted to hunt again, but I decided he had had enough for
one day and took him home.

If you walk up doves, be sure that you do it near enough to
water so that you can cool a dog that becomes overheated. If there
is no water nearby, don't use your dog. The risk just isn't worth
taking.

Many people, especially those who run their retrievers in
field trials, are reluctant to hunt pheasants with their dogs unless
they keep them at heel except to fetch downed birds. They believe
that to let their dogs actually get out and put birds up will require
that the dog be taught to quarter (zigzag) like a springer spaniel,
and it is generally agreed that this will weaken the clean, straight
lines a retriever is supposed to take to the marks and especially to
the blind retrieves in field trials. Quartering to falls and to blinds
in field trials is a definite no-no, since it disturbs too much cover.
Field trials are for nonslip retrievers—those that stay at heel until
sent to retrieve. Most retriever field trial people insist that if you
want a dog to quarter in front of you for pheasants, you should
either buy a springer or use a retriever that does not compete in
field trials.

I must agree that it is nearly impossible to train a dog to quarter for pheasants and to run clean, straight lines to blind retrieves.
I do not agree that this makes it impossible to let your field trial retriever flush pheasants for you, however. I have worked out a sys-
tem, using the whistle commands taught to field trial retrievers,
that will make an excellent pheasant flusher out of a field trial retriever and not damage the dog's competitive career at all.

When I hunt pheasants, I give my dog a release command.
(All dogs should have one command that tells them they are free

to do what they please until further notice). My dog will start to follow his nose, seeking game. If he wanders too far in front of me, I simply blow one sharp blast on the whistle, which to a field trial retriever means "Stop, turn around, sit down, and look at me." My dog sits there until I come closer to him, at which time I give him the release command again. If he runs too far to either side, I simply blow the come-in whistle. When he returns to within proper range, I give him the release command again. With the two whistle signals and the release command, I can keep him hunting close enough so that I can shoot, or at least shoot at, any bird he flushes. He does not quarter; he just follows his nose, which is the best thing for him to do anyway. I make no effort to direct his hunting pattern other than to keep him close enough to me all the time. Naturally, if he is on a bird when he reaches the limit, I speed up and follow him rather than stop or recall him, although I have stopped my dogs when they were trailing birds so that I could keep up with them.

Personally I prefer that the dog break to flush in this kind of pheasant hunting. Many disagree with me on that, I know, but I

Figure 8.   A stylish Labrador is sent for a marked retrieve.

like to have the dog "on top" of the pheasant when it hits the ground. Pheasants are such runners that I hate to handicap the dog any more than I have to. Besides, pheasants flush high, so there is no danger of the dog being hit with stray pellets, even if he is right under the bird when it is shot. It is a rare pheasant that flies low after the flush, and that rare bird goes free when I am hunting. I won't risk shooting my dog.

Quail are a different story. They fly low and in every direction. If you want to hunt quail with a retriever, you had better be certain that the dog is steady to wing and shot. Personally I prefer pointing breeds for quail, but even these should be steady. Could a person train a dog to be steady on quail and break on pheasants? I wouldn't say it is impossible, but it would take more time and effort than I am willing to put into it. It is better to use different dogs for the two different jobs.

FIELD TRIAL HANDLING

Single marked retrieves are rare in licensed trials, but they are common in puppy and gundog stakes at fun trials.

The handling of the dog on a single mark starts before you get the dog to the line. It is important that you heel your dog to the line along a path that allows the dog to locate the guns *before* arriving at the line. Sometimes it is difficult to see the guns from the line, because of the sun or a patch of cover or any of several other problems. Seeing to it that your dog already knows where the guns are will minimize the effect of such difficulties. I remember two trials in which the judges deliberately set the line up using trees to block the view so that the dogs could not see the guns from the line. I think this is very bad judging, but it is not against the rules as long as the dog can see the bird as it falls.

Once you reach the line, you should position your dog facing the guns. Let the dog take all the time necessary to get comfortable and to "lock in" on the guns before you signal that you are ready. If the rules of the stake allow it, use a lead or belt cord to prevent your dog from breaking. No matter how steady you think your dog is, remember that all dogs will break now and then. You will get no extra points for not using allowable forms of restraint, but you will be dropped from competition if your dog breaks, so why risk it?

After the bird is thrown, your dog must remain at the line until the judge tells you, usually by calling your number, that you may send the dog out. Although you may not send your dog before this, you are not required to send him immediately after it. Allow your dog a second or two to concentrate on the location of the fall, and then send him. After you work with your retriever for a while, you will be able to tell by his intensity when he is ready to be sent.

Once in a fun trial puppy stake, I saw a judge give a friend of his a good lesson in not sending her dog as soon as her number was called. Normally judges don't do this sort of thing, even in fun trials, but in this instance I think it was helpful. The handler's number was thirteen. In each of the first two series (or tests), as soon as the judge said "Thirteen," the handler said "Back!" It was almost like one sound—"Thirteenback," with no pause at all. In the third series, the judge didn't say "Thirteen." Instead, he said "Back!" The handler, in her anxiety to launch her dog, hollered "Thirteen." As soon as the word was past her lips, she realized that she had said the wrong thing, and she put both hands up as if she were trying to shove the word back into her mouth. Her dog did the test very well, in spite of the mix-up in commands, and the woman learned a lesson.

Had she taken her time and let her dog really lock in on the mark before she sent him, she would not have said "Thirteen" instead of "Back!" The precise word used is not all that important, of course, but the handler's slip of the tongue indicates how anxious she was to get her dog off and running. She was conditioned to say "Back!" as soon as her number was called, so when the judge said "Back!" unexpectedly, she instinctively called her number.

When your dog picks up the bird, blow the come-in whistle. Be sure, however, that the dog really has the bird before you blow the signal. I have seen dogs obediently return without the bird because the handler tooted too soon. See that the bird is in the dog's mouth; then blow the whistle. Just because your dog sticks his head into the cover near where you think the bird is, you should not assume that he has it. The dog could be smelling an old fall near the bird. The only purpose in blowing the come-in whistle is to remind your dog where you are. The retriever may have had quite a hunt before finding the bird and may not be sure where you are. If you always blow the whistle right after you see your retriever pick up the bird, your dog will form the habit of heading for the sound of the whistle immediately instead of wandering around looking for you. Then, too, sometimes part of the bird will be covering the dog's eyes so that he cannot see you.

When your dog returns to the line, take the bird from him as smoothly as possible. In stakes where delivery to hand is required, the dog should be trained to sit at heel to deliver. At the sit, grasp the bird's head or feet, whichever is closer to you, and command the dog to release it. A properly trained dog will not only let loose but will also back his head away from the bird. It is a mistake to pull a bird from a dog's mouth, even after the dog has released it. Such an action tempts the dog to grab for the bird, and this can lead to stickiness (refusal to release the bird on command). Instead, train your dog to release and back away slightly so that the bird drops out of his mouth. Of course, you should have a firm grip on the bird to keep it from hitting the ground.

Put the bird on your other side immediately, to prevent your dog from trying to jump at it—an annoying habit that can lead to more serious problems. Get the bird out of the dog's reach as quickly as you can.

In stakes not requiring delivery to hand, there is normally a requirement that the dog bring the bird across the line. To encourage this, move back a little as your dog approaches the line. If you move toward the dog—and here I am talking about the very young, relatively untrained puppy—he will be inclined to stop and possibly drop the bird before reaching the line.

Give the bird to the judge as soon as you get it. Then thank the judges and depart. Always thank the judges, even if you think they are doing a terrible job of setting up tests. They are working without pay, after all, and they are trying to do a good job. Someday you will have the opportunity to act as a judge, and then you will find out how difficult the job is. Judges, like the officials in all competitive events, receive much criticism and little appreciation.

After you have thanked them, heel your dog away as quickly as possible. Nothing good can come from staying near the line any longer than necessary. Your dog could get into all sorts of trouble there—like finding the bird pile behind the judges, or jumping at the bird hanging from the judge's hand, or lifting his leg on the judge's boots. Why take a chance? Get the dog out of there! If you have questions, return later without your dog to ask them.

Training Tests

The rest of this chapter is devoted to training test diagrams and explanations of single marked retrieves. These tests show how terrain, cover, and wind affect the dog's work. While all these tests are singles, the environmental factors have similar influence on the marks in doubles and triples. Each mark in a multiple marking test is itself a single mark, so what is said here about terrain, cover, and wind applies to all marking tests.

No lengths are indicated on any of the test diagrams because several considerations govern the lengths you should use for each test you give your dog.

One major factor in determining test length is your own goals for your dog. If you aspire to field trial immortality, you will run your dog on a great variety of lengths, from quite short to perhaps 200 yards. If you want only to earn a working certificate, you will probably limit your tests to the lengths your national breed club requires for the certificate. If you are training your dog strictly for hunting, you will want to run your tests from very short to as much as twice the length of your typical fall in the duck blind or in the field. Why twice as long? Well, think about the birds that set their wings and sail before they come down, even though they have been hit hard. In the past, you have probably lost a lot of those birds. Now, with your dog, you should get most of them.

Another significant factor in deciding how long a test distance should be is the experience level of your dog when you run the test. Don't bewilder young puppies with lengths that they might be afraid even to attempt. In all your training, try to build confidence through trial and success. Extend the distances slowly, and let your dog enjoy success throughout the process.

Visibility is another important consideration. If the terrain, cover, or background is such that the dog cannot see the bird at a certain distance, then don't use that distance. Obviously, it would be foolish to attempt a mark of a certain length if an intervening hill would keep the dog from seeing the fall. Not quite so obvious is the situation in which the line is on top of a hill and the mark is on the slope of the same hill. It will be difficult for the dog to see such a fall if the hill is quite steep. The location should be moved farther out onto the flat beyond the base of the hill for better visibility. Squat down and look at the situation from the dog's point of view to see what I mean. If the background is quite dark—a row of tall trees, for example—the dog may have trouble picking out the bird or dummy when it is thrown if the distance is very great. Remember that dogs are color-blind, so spotting a red dummy against a green background is not as easy for them as it is for us.

No matter what you are training your dog for, vary the length of the throws frequently. Dogs learn by rote, and if you always give the same length tests, your dog will form a habit of running just that far before starting to hunt for the bird. Some beginning trainers seem to think that once their dogs have mastered a given length and moved on, they should never have to go back to that distance again. This is not so. Lengthen the distance gradually at first, but only to let your dog gain confidence. You must continue to use the shorter tests even after the dog is comfortable with the longest test you intend to give. I once saw a dog win a fun trial puppy stake in which the test distances were very long and then fail in the first series of a puppy stake the following week at another fun trial in which the test distance was not more than 20 yards. The dog ran past the mark and kept going until he was about 100 yards out. Then he started hunting. That dog was about ten months old, and large. Later a little four-month-old puppy came to the line and did the test beautifully.

WIND CONSIDERATIONS

A simple single marked retrieve on land under four different wind conditions is shown in Figure 9.

Figure 9–A shows the test with the wind blowing from the line to the mark—a downwind situation. For the dog to be able to use his nose, he will have to drive a little deep and work back in to the bird. This is the preferred condition for most marks, because it eliminates any help for the dog until he runs to or past the bird. If the dog doesn't "step on it"—that is, run right to the bird and pick it up—he must move on out past it if he is to complete the test. Hunting short (not getting all the way to the bird) is a serious fault, and this wind direction penalizes the dog that hunts short. Consequently, this wind direction is preferred for most marking tests.

The same test with a crosswind blowing from the guns to the mark appears in Figure 9–B. Normally a dog will tend to drift a little with the wind; in this case, he will swing wide of the mark away from the gun. As soon as he gets as deep as the bird is, he will pick up its scent. For single marked retrieves this is a very friendly wind, one that helps the dog considerably. It can be friendly or unfriendly in multiple marking tests, depending on where the other falls are. If one of them is so positioned that the dog will get into its area as he drifts with the wind, it will be a tougher test; if not, it will be easier.

Figure 9–C shows the same test with a crosswind blowing from the bird to the gun. A dog is likely to drift behind the gun with this wind; it really isn't the crime that some people seem to think it is for a dog to go behind the gun as long as he is in the area of the fall. One problem can arise behind the gun, however—a problem that the dog will not run into anywhere else—scent from the bird sack at the gun's feet. That bird sack will be closer to the dog than the fall will be, so the dog will pick up the sack's scent

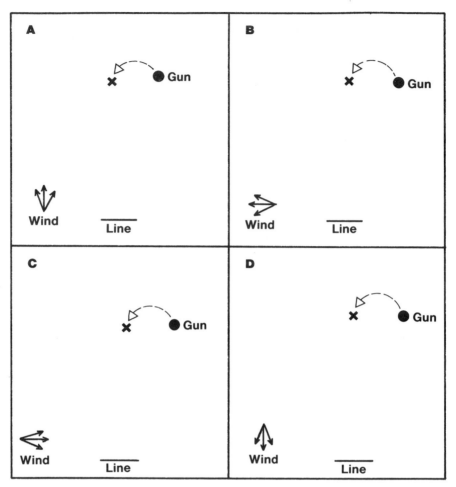

Figure 9.   Wind considerations.

first. Some inexperienced dogs become so interested in the bird
sack that they do not complete the test. Under this wind condition, I once saw a derby dog in a licensed trial—and he was handled by a pro, too—climb up on top of a stack of bird crates full of
pheasants and try to dig his way in. I'm sure that the pro gave that
particular dog some extra lessons in staying away from the guns
right after that. Having your dog trained to stay away from the gun
is the key to working in this wind. One solution is to have the gun
swing a whip around every time the dog tries to get near the bird
sack during training sessions. If the dog keeps coming, he runs
into the whip and gets stung; if he backs off, he doesn't get hurt.
The gun should never chase the dog off or shout at him. He
should just stand still between the dog and the bird sack and
swing the whip. The dog should be frightened only of the whip,
never of the gun; a dog that is afraid of the gun will sometimes re-

fuse to get near enough to him to make a retrieve. Man-shyness is always bad.

Figure 9–D shows the test with a wind blowing from the mark to the line. This is the simplest wind of all; it almost pulls the dog right to the bird from the moment he leaves the line. Nevertheless, it is probably the worst wind to use, especially with young dogs. The problem is that it encourages the dog to quarter (zigzag) his way out to the bird, following the moving scent as it shifts this way and that on the ever-changing wind. Retrievers should run straight to their marks; dogs that quarter are severely penalized. If young dogs are given enough into-the-wind marks, they may form a lifelong habit of quartering to every fall, regardless of wind direction. For this reason, you should probably not give a retrieve into the wind until your dog is reasonably advanced in the work, perhaps not until he is doing simple blind retrieves. He won't attempt to quarter on his lines to blinds if he has never done it on marks.

To summarize the use of wind directions in setting up tests, I recommend that you use straight downwind marks wherever possible. Do not set up tests in crosswinds unless you have a specific reason, and never set up an upwind mark, at least not for a young dog. When in doubt, use a downwind direction (Figure 9–A).

ROAD HAZARDS

Figure 10–C illustrates a single mark in which the gun is positioned on the side of a road nearer to the line while the fall is on the far side of the road. This gives some dogs serious problems. They tend to stay on the near side of the road and hunt instead of driving on across as they should. The road acts as a boundary for them; the fact that the gun is on the near side also encourages them to hunt short.

The road here is nothing more than a car or tractor trail through a field rather than a public thoroughfare. It is dangerous to work across any road on which the dog might encounter traffic.

The heavier the cover, the more the dog will be inclined to stay on the near side of the road. For this reason, the dog should be started in light to moderate cover when training for this test.

The temptation to stay on the near side is not as strong if the gun is on the far side of the road, too, as in Figure 10–B. With the road close to the line, as in 10–A, the problem is greatly simplified. For this reason, it is best to start the dog on roads with the test set up as in 10–A and then gradually toughen it up to something like

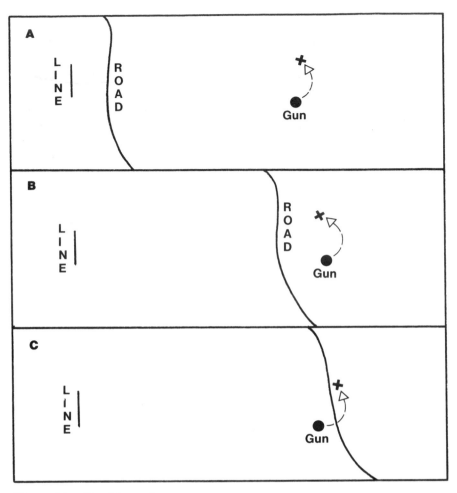

Figure 10.   Road hazards.

10–B and finally to 10–C. That way the dog makes progress without many failures. In this mark, confidence is everything. A dog that becomes accustomed to it gradually, without many failures, will learn it quickly and easily. A dog, especially a young one, that fails too often will become bewildered and may even stop retrieving altogether. You don't need that problem. Approach this test slowly, and the dog's confidence will keep pace with the work you want to accomplish. That is the fastest way to train a dog in most things.

Another technique that builds confidence in a young dog is "salting" the area of the fall. Put several dummies out in the area before you run the dog on the test; that way he will find a dummy if he gets into the salted area. If only one dummy is out there, the dog may miss it and suffer a failure. It is important that he learn that he will find a dummy if he gets to the area, so have plenty of them out there for him in the early stages of training.

Do not salt the area if you are using pigeons (or any other kind of real bird), for the dog may try to bring in two or three of them at the same time. This could start a hard-mouth problem. It is best to use dummies until salting is no longer necessary.

One more point: after your dog is handling this test well, occasionally throw a mark on the near side of the road, to be certain that he won't come to think that he must always cross any road he comes to. You are trying to train him to ignore the road, not to use it as a point of reference.

SIDEWINDER

The mark shown in Figure 11 can be anything from "a portion of pastry" to a real character builder, depending on the wind direction. The bird is thrown up the side of a hill, and the dog has to run along the side of that hill all the way to the fall. Most dogs will tend to fade downhill to some degree as they go along, and this makes the difficulty of the test dependent on the wind. If the wind is such that drifting downhill helps the dog, then this is an easy test; if the wind makes it more difficult to scent the bird, the dog can face real difficulty.

Wind A, which blows across the test area and down the hill, will make it easier to scent the bird if the dog drifts downhill. Wind B is not much different, except that the dog must drive a little past the fall before scenting it. Both wind A and wind B make this a very easy test.

Wind C, blowing straight downwind from the line, is another matter. Dogs that drift downhill will not get any scent unless they drive back up the hill after they pass the fall. Most dogs will not do that. They will hunt the entire valley instead.

Wind D is the real sidewinder in this test. It blows the scent up over the top of the hill, forcing the dogs to go against their natural tendency to fade downhill as they go out. The dogs must dig for the high ground if they are to find the bird at all.

How do you train for this test? Rerun, rerun, rerun. Just to keep yourself from getting too upset, assume that your dog is not going to do too well the first time, and help him any way you can. Be sure that he completes the test the first time, even if you and the gun have to work together to show him where the bird is (assuming he doesn't find it on his own). Once he has completed the test, even with a lot of help, he knows where the bird is. Rerun him on it immediately, while the location of the bird is still fresh in his mind. This will give him a better picture of the fall from

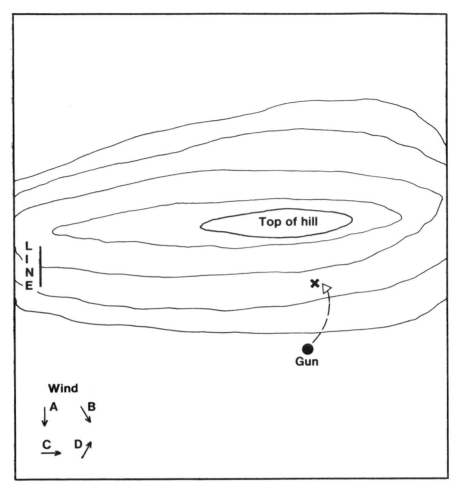

Figure 11. The Sidewinder.

the line. He will probably pin it the second time, but if he doesn't, don't get excited; help him again. Eventually, he will see the light: "Oh, I get it, boss. It's up on the side of the hill all the time."

Once the dog has the idea, whether on the first or fifth attempt, rerun the test a couple more times to cement the idea in.

Some dogs have a more serious problem in this kind of training than others. If yours is an easy one, be thankful. If not, don't be too distressed by it, and above all, don't lose your temper and start punishing him. Stay calm, help him out as often as necessary, and then rerun, rerun, rerun. It works. Getting angry doesn't.

One point should be mentioned concerning reruns: don't overdo them during any one training session. I have seen people do reruns until their dogs were exhausted. This accomplishes nothing except to make the dog dislike the work. If your dog becomes noticeably tired before he has had sufficient reruns, let him rest for half an hour and work another dog or help other handlers with their dogs. Then bring your dog out again for a rerun. If you decide that he has really had enough for the day, stop training and bring your dog back to the same test the next day. There is no rule that says your dog has to master a test in one training session.

OPTICAL ILLUSION

Figure 12 shows a fairly innocent-looking mark that can present the inattentive dog with serious problems. The line is at the bottom of a fairly steep hill, and the gun is about halfway up the

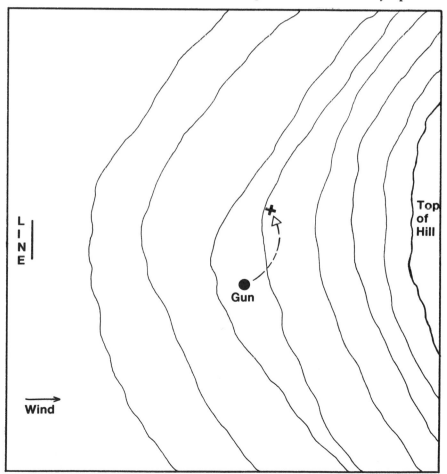

Figure 12. Optical illusion.

hill. The wind can be either straight away or quartering away from the line.

It is imperative that the bird "break the horizon" when it is thrown—that is, it must be tossed high enough so that the dog sees it silhouetted against the sky. This is what causes the problem. The dog sees the bird rising against the sky and then falling back to earth, but where exactly does the bird actually touch the ground? The inattentive dog will lose sight of it when it stops being silhouetted against the sky and will mark it at that spot, which is way up on top of the hill. The dog that is really concentrating on the bird will follow its descent against the darker background after it loses its backlighting and will mark it correctly.

Dogs usually do either very well or very poorly on this test. They will either "pin" the bird and make the task look ridiculously simple or they will head straight for the top of the hill and do all of their hunting up there. Inexperienced puppies and head-swinging derby dogs seem to have the most trouble with this test, the derbies especially when looking for the memory bird in a marked double retrieve. A diversion flier intensifies the problem for the derby dog.

Even the all-age dog can have difficulty with this kind of mark if it is part of a triple and the guns retire.

The secret of training your dog to do this test is to rerun, rerun, rerun. Help him find the bird until he understands where it is actually falling and then rerun him a few more times to be sure. Naturally, you should not rerun your dog too often without giving him a rest—overnight if he is really too tired. Dogs don't learn much when they are exhausted.

DOWNHILL MARKS

Three distinct tests appear in Figure 13. The line is in the same place for each test, but the guns are positioned differently.

The test with gun A is a straight downhill mark. Most dogs tend to overrun this fall and then not return back up the slope after they reach the flat ground. The only cure is to rerun, rerun, rerun, as in so many tests that present terrain problems. Time and experience will enable the dog to understand the test.

The exercise with gun B is a two-level test. From the top of the hill, the dog gets a good look at the fall, but the terrain just doesn't look the same to him after he has run down the hill to the bird. Most dogs lose their marks the first time they run this test. They might go anywhere once they get to the level ground; they're

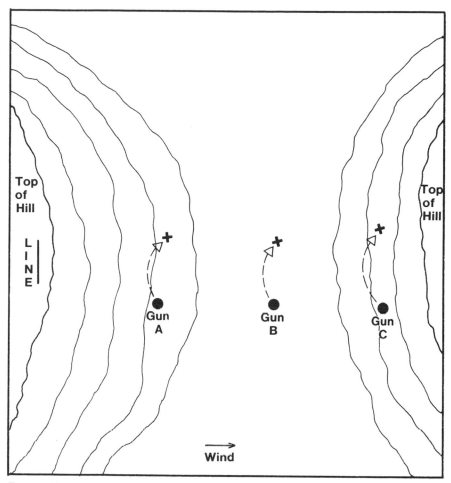

Figure 13. Downhill marks.

lost. It takes many reruns for the dog to get his bearings down in the valley. The problem is that the test looks so easy from the line that many trainers grow impatient with their dogs too quickly.

The test with gun C is a downhill–uphill exercise. A dog should be pretty far along in his marks before you throw this one at him. Even then, you will do best to start with the line down in the valley and move it back as the dog progresses. If he cannot handle the test with the line down below, there is no way he will succeed with it on top of the hill.

BROKEN-FIELD RUNNING

In the test shown in Figure 14 a strip of very heavy cover runs between the line and the fall. Both the line and the fall are in

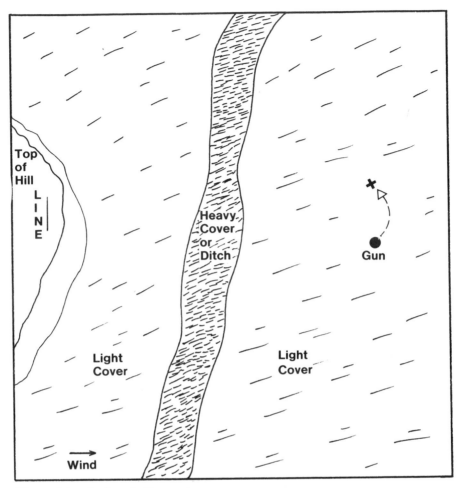

Figure 14. Broken-field running

light cover. The line is on a slight incline, high enough so that the dog can see the mark over the heavy cover patch.

The problem in this test is that the dog loses visual contact with the fall as he plows through the heavy cover. If a dog can look at the spot where the bird fell while he is running to it, his chances of mismarking are greatly reduced. Anything that breaks this visual contact makes the mark that much tougher. If the cover is so dense that the dog has to zigzag through it, he may come out the other side on a different line altogether. This makes it even more difficult for him to get his bearings again.

In starting to work on this test, it is a good idea to use big white plastic dummies, so that the dog will see them more readily. Salting the area with several dummies will also help. These techniques build confidence by ensuring success.

Of course, there is no substitute for the three R's: rerun, rerun, rerun, with adequate rest between.

An interesting variation of this test is seen when a ditch is used instead of the heavy cover. The principle is the same: the dog loses visual contact with the fall as he runs through the ditch, and then must reorient himself when he comes out the other side.

BASIC WATER MARKS

Figure 15–A shows a simple water mark in which the bird is thrown into a patch of cover in the water. Figure 15–B shows the same test, but here the bird is thrown into the cover on land.

Most dogs get too much work on the type of test shown in

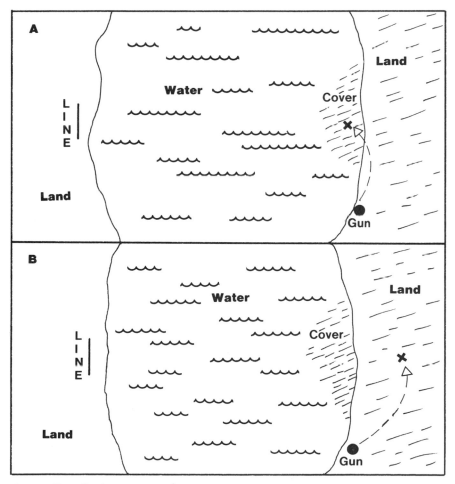

Figure 15. Basic water marks.

15–B and not nearly enough on the other one, in which the bird is actually in the water. There are a number of reasons for this. First, it is not always easy to find water with cover in it. Second and more important, however, it is much more difficult to act as the gun in a test where the bird has to fall in the water. The bird must be more precisely thrown, for one thing. Then, too, if a dog fails the test and has to be helped, the gun must wade in and pick the bird up. (The gun also has to do this after every bad throw.) Somehow it is just very difficult actually to get around to using the 15–A form of the test very often.

The test shown in 15–B is another matter, however. There is no problem finding a place, and the test causes no inconvenience for the gun; we all run lots of these. Our dogs show it, too. They tend to be bank-runners (why stay in the water when the birds are always on land?), and even when in the water, they are always looking for shortcuts to the nearest land. They will fail most field-trial tests in which a bird is thrown into cover in the water, because they have been trained not to start hunting until they reach land. Right? Yes, that is what we are teaching them.

I have actually seen dogs swim past live shackled ducks in open water to land and hunt the cover on shore! Of course, the duck was motionless and perhaps looked like a decoy, and it is true that the dogs swam by on the wrong side of the wind. It is also true, however, that they had their "hunting switches" turned off while they were in the water.

The point of all this is that you should give your dog plenty of the type A tests, perhaps even more than you give him of the type B. If you want him to love the water, let him find lots of birds there.

BOAT PEOPLE

Figure 16 shows a simple water mark thrown from a boat. For some reason, certain dogs are reluctant to swim near a boat— at least until they have been around boats for a while. If you have such a dog, take a little time to get him used to boats before you ask him to retrieve a bird thrown from one.

If possible, start this familiarization on land. Pull a little boat into the back yard, and let your dog become accustomed to it at his leisure. Don't try to encourage him in any way. Just leave dog and boat alone together for a few days. After that, heel him around it; when he can handle that, climb into the boat and coax the dog into joining you; when he does, just sit there and pet him for a

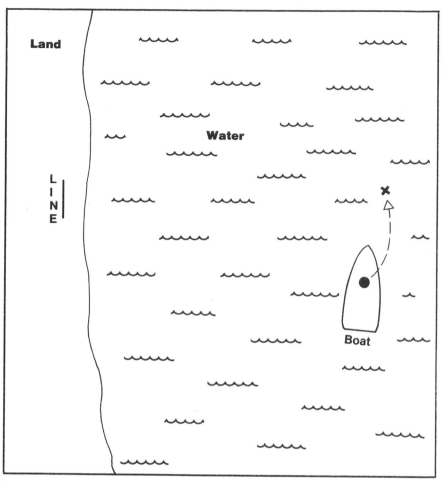

Figure 16. Boat people.

while. Next, stand in the boat, throw a dummy out, and have him retrieve it to you there in the boat.

When the dog is no longer afraid of the boat on land, take him for a ride in it on calm water. Then beach it and have him do a few short water and land retrieves from it. Finally, leave him on shore while you row out a short distance. Then call the dog to you and let him swim behind the boat as you row it for some distance. After a while, stop and help him aboard. His fear of boats should be gone after all this. Incidentally, having a dog swim behind a rowed boat is excellent exercise—for both of you.

A boat is a fine training aid; it allows you to throw marks in places a long way from shore. If you can find any patches of cover out in the middle of a pond, use them this way. Frequently finding birds a long way from shore improves a dog's attitude toward water.

Early in Duffy's career, I was invited to hunt with some friends in a place where we would be shooting from a boat. I accepted gladly and then realized that I had never given Duffy any exposure to boats. To make matters worse, I didn't even own a boat at that time, and I was not able to borrow one until the night before the hunt. I dragged the borrowed boat into my yard before supper and let Duffy become acquainted with it while I ate. We hadn't been living in our house very long at the time and did not know our neighbors at all well.

As I sat eating supper, it occurred to me that Duffy could probably use a refresher course in ignoring decoys, too. After dinner I put Duffy in his run and spread a dozen mallard decoys near where the boat stood. Then I dug a frozen duck out of the freezer. (All retriever trainers have frozen ducks, feathers and all, in their freezers.) I had one of my kids toss the duck into the yard past the decoys while I stood in the boat with the dog, and then I had Duffy retrieve the duck through the decoys. We did that until I was sure Duffy was having no problems with either the boat or the decoys.

The only problem was that it was raining quite hard that evening. I was wearing my camo (camouflage) raincoat. I have often wondered, but have been afraid to ask, what our new neighbors thought of all this—me standing in a boat in my back yard, wearing a camo raincoat, with a spread of decoys all over the yard, having my dog retrieve a frozen mallard thrown by one of my kids— all in a driving rainstorm. I suppose that this was one of the saner things they have seen me do with my dogs in the back yard through the years.

STUMP JUMPING

Figure 17 shows a simple water mark with some hazards in the form of stumps and limbs sticking up around the fall. It looks like a good piece of bass water, actually.

Some dogs sail right through this test the first time, and some seem to spook at the sight of all that timber out there. Some will climb right over a limb; others will detour around it. All dogs need some exposure to this kind of water, however, for it is used in field trials and it is very common in actual hunting situations.

If your dog spooks when he sees the stumps and limbs, you might be wise to stop training for a while and just wade around in the water yourself, encouraging the dog to follow. Let him get comfortable this way before you ask him to retrieve in this kind of place.

One thing to be very careful of in setting up this kind of test

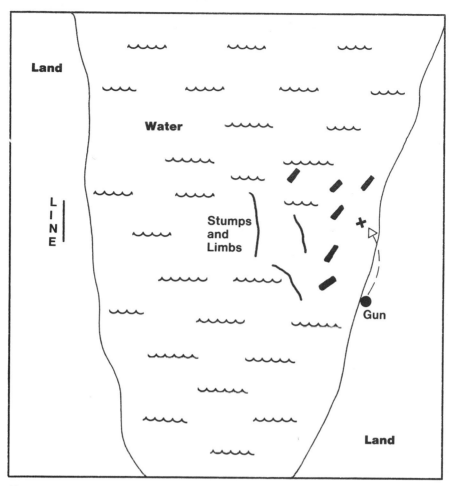

Figure 17. Stump jumping.

is submerged stumps on the side of the lake where you put the line. A dog can really hurt himself on these as he runs or jumps into the water. Check all over the area of entry for any unseen hazards before you run your dog. Not only is there the danger of injury, but also the dog that has hit a submerged stump or other object will not be eager to jump into the water anywhere again soon. Such an experience could be the start of water-shyness, a serious problem for a retriever.

DECOY HAZARDS

In hunting, decoys are set out to attract ducks; in field trials they are used to attract dogs. Dogs are supposed to be trained to ignore decoys in making retrieves, so licensed trials require every dog that places to be tested on decoys at least once.

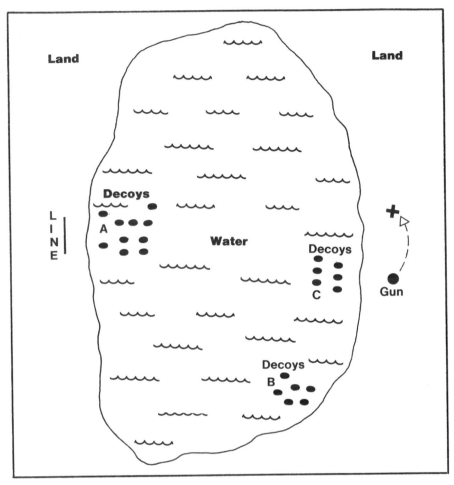

Figure 18. Decoy hazards.

Decoy spreads in trials are different from those in actual hunting. In the first place, not very many are used in trials: usually only three to six. In the second place, the decoys are positioned differently. There are really only three places that decoys are likely to be in a trial.

They may be right in front of the line, as in Figure 18–A. So placed, they will prove whether a dog has been trained to leave them alone, and little else, especially in a single marked retrieve. In a double or triple, the decoys may mislead a dog that has a faulty memory. Their primary purpose in position 18–A, however, is just to test the dog's basic response to decoys: will he or will he not ignore them?

Decoys in Figure 18–B are normally only used in multiple marks. Their purpose is not so much to test the dog's reactions to decoys as it is to see whether or not the dog has properly marked the memory birds. The dog that has trouble remembering a memory bird is likely to start toward the decoys, thinking that maybe the memory bird will be around there someplace. Once a dog does this, there is little chance that he will complete the test without help from the handler. Any time decoys are set up a long way from the line and a long way from any of the marks, they are there to draw the dogs away from the marks.

Decoys in Figure 18–C will test the dog's reaction to them in the area of the fall. Some dogs will ignore them close to the line but play with them if they have to swim some distance before reaching them. The mark may be thrown behind the decoys, as in this drawing, or right in among them. Either way, the dog should ignore them and find the bird. Decoys in this position will actually help the dog that has forgotten where the memory bird is. If you set up too many memory birds this way, however, your dog will face trouble in a trial when they are set up like those in Figure 18–B.

Training dogs to ignore decoys should be started on land, of course. Toss out a dozen or so somewhere in the yard, and then heel your dog through them. Every time the dog attempts to sniff a decoy, say "No!" and give a sharp jerk with the lead. No matter how good your dog is at heeling, keep the lead on for this exercise. After the dog has learned not to touch the decoys while heeling, give a short retrieve off to one side of them—not in them or past them, yet, please. Do this in several different directions around decoys. If the dog attempts to go near the decoys on the way out or back, yell "No," grab the end of the lead (which should be dragging), and pull the dog back away from them. After your dog is able to complete these retrieves without bothering the blocks, toss the dummy directly on the other side of the decoys and send the dog after it. By now, you should have no problem. Later, toss the dummy right in the middle of the spread.

Do all of this on land, right in your own yard. It is a good idea to move the decoys from one place to another as you progress. If you don't, your dog might get the idea that it is that one spot in the yard rather than the decoys that you don't want him going near. The canine mind works in strange ways.

After the yard work is done, move to shallow water—shallow so that you can wade out to your dog if necessary. Only after the dog has demonstrated an understanding of decoys in a shallow area can you safely try working in deep water.

You may ask why you can't skip the dry land and start in shallow water. There is a good reason for starting on land. You will have to do most of your correcting in whatever place you start. If that is in water, the dog may develop a bad attitude toward the wet stuff, and this can cause serious problems. Why risk it?

One more point is important: when using decoys in water, be sure to set them up so that the danger of your dog becoming tangled in the cords is minimal. Use short cords and leave enough space between blocks so that your dog is not forced to swim too close to any of them. Getting tangled in decoy lines can be a frightening experience and can affect a dog's attitude toward water.

THE DRUNKEN SAILOR

Figure 19 illustrates a land-water-land-water-land single mark. I call it "the drunken sailor" because the first few times they try it, many dogs just stumble around out there, sometimes on land, sometimes in the water.

The problem is that, from the line, the dog cannot see the second stretch of water. Most places in which this test can be set up are on rolling hills, so that the middle area of land is high enough to block the dog's view of the second stretch of water. The dog sees only a mark thrown on land across a cove. He swims that cove and starts hunting for the bird on the middle area of land. Even if he discovers the second cove, he assumes that the bird can be no farther away, for he saw only one cove from the line. Even with the gun standing in plain sight and wearing a white jacket, most dogs will not swim the second stretch of water.

The problem is complicated by the fact that the dog lost visual contact with the fall as he swam the first cove; that middle stretch of land blocked his view all the time he was in the water. When he reaches land, everything looks different than it did from the line. The dog becomes confused and just mills around like a drunken sailor.

You can handle a mature dog through this test the first time. The younger dog—or any dog that you cannot handle through the exercise—requires a different approach. The important thing is to prevent the dog from losing confidence by avoiding failure. Probably the surest way of doing this is first to place the line on the middle stretch of land rather than back where it is in the diagram. From the middle stretch the dog can see the second body of water—the only water between him and the mark. This is a simple test, and your dog should have no trouble with it. Run it from the center stretch of land two or three times to be sure that the dog can handle it.

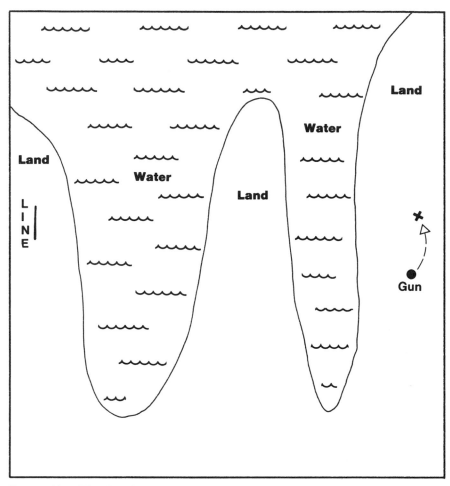

Figure 19. The drunken sailor.

Then, after resting for a while, move the line back to where it is in the diagram and run the test again. Now your dog should have no problem at all with the exercise. If he does, you will know that you didn't give him enough work with the line on the middle peninsula. Go back and do some more retrieves from there. Eventually the dog will get the picture and will then be able to do the test from the original line.

This training is not unlike the across-the-road test on land (Figure 10). In that test the dog tends to regard the road as an outer limit until he has been trained to go across it. He sees the hidden body of water in the same way.

Run this test in as many locations as you can find. It really forces your dog to mark the birds where they are rather than where they might be.

I have seen many all-age dogs fail this test as a single marked retrieve. If it is made one of the memory birds in a multiple marking test, very few dogs of any age will get through it without being handled, and those that do deserve special credit.

ANGLE IN

Figure 20 shows a test that requires the retriever to enter the water at an angle. A dog that fails to do so will move along the shoreline (run the bank) and will probably get lost in the heavy cover. Frequently, a dog that does this will never complete the retrieve but will hunt the cover instead of going into the water.

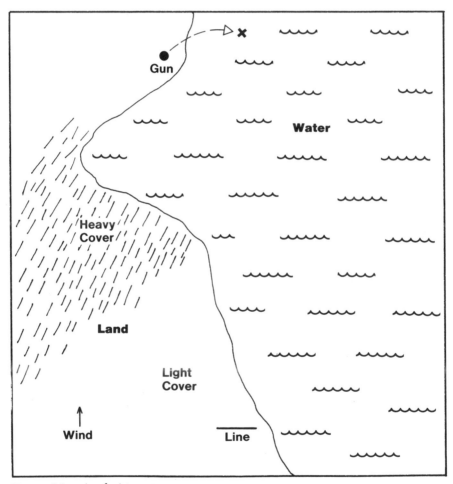

Figure 20.   Angle in.

In many angled-entry marks it really doesn't matter whether the dog runs the bank or not, but in this one such a dog will be penalized. In field trials, dogs are expected to handle all angled entries properly. The dog that does so is a better-trained retriever and can cope with more problems than can the bank runner. In hunting it seldom matters whether the dog runs the bank or takes to the water, and many hunters believe that it is not worth the effort to train their dogs to take good angles into water. That is a choice each individual dog owner has to make.

If you want your dog to take angles into the water, keep a few things in mind.

First, don't start this training when your dog is too young. Let the dog develop confidence in water work first. Generally, you will do better to wait until your retriever is handling doubles in water comfortably. If you start any sooner there is the danger of turning him sour on water work altogether. The younger he is when this happens, the more permanent the damage can be.

Second, no matter how well your dog is doing on doubles, go back to single marks for this training. Look at the situation this way: a dog that cannot handle angled entries on singles will have no success in handling them on doubles. If you push him too fast, he may quit on you. If he does, you will have to go back several squares and start again.

Most important, train for this test under the guidance of a competent professional. The forms of correction required are rather delicate, in that any misuse can cause serious damage. Do not depend on yourself or on an amateur friend. Go to a competent pro.

ANGLE OUT

In the mark shown in Figure 21, the dog that tries to land too soon—on the first island instead of the second one—will probably never complete the test. The fact that there are indeed two islands may not be all that apparent to a dog standing at the line. The dog may think that he is in the proper place as soon as he lands on the first island. Even if he can see from the line that there are two islands, the dog that lands on the first one will normally hunt it and fail to drive on to the second island. The tip of the first island becomes a boundary for such a dog.

The dog that lands on the first island is said to be "cheating." This is always penalized in field trials, but in many hunting situa-

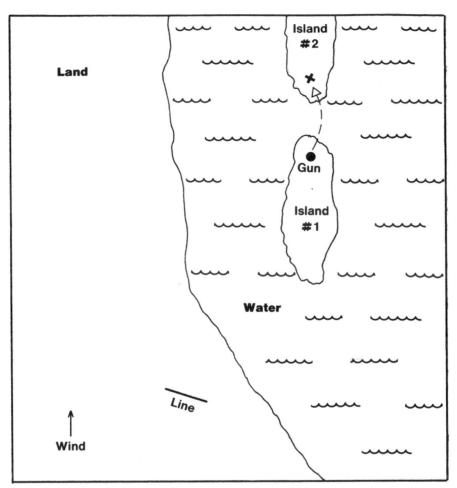

Figure 21.   Angle out.

tions it really doesn't matter all that much. In this particular test, however, finding the right island will mean the difference between failure and success.

Each individual retriever owner must decide whether it is worth the effort to train a dog not to cheat in water exits. Those who choose to train for this test must take the same precautions as they did for the angle-in training (Figure 20). Don't start until the dog is well along in water doubles. In fact, wait until he can handle angles in before starting angles out. Also, go back to single retrieves to teach this, and above all, follow the guidance of a competent professional.

2. *DOUBLE MARKED RETRIEVES*

Training Tips

A double marked retrieve is a test in which two birds are thrown in two different locations and the dog is expected to retrieve them one at a time. Since this is a marking test, the dog is allowed to see the falls so that he can mark them. Dogs typically retrieve the last bird thrown first, and the first bird thrown last. For this reason, the first bird thrown is called the memory bird and the last one thrown is called the diversion. The dog has to retain the mark for the memory bird while searching for the diversion. As you can see, a double mark tests not only the dog's marking ability but also his memory.

Doubles occur on land, in water, and in combinations of land and water. You should allow your dog's water work to lag behind the land work, just as you did in single marks. The reasons are the same: water is the more difficult medium for a dog, and you cannot get to him easily to help or to correct when he is in the water. You should allow his switchproofing (see below) to lag in water. I have often seen people—to their sorrow—set up a switching test in water for a dog that has not been completely switchproofed on land. Such a dog will switch, and the handler can do nothing about it except stand there and yell in Technicolor. Many serious switching problems have been caused this way.

Some trainers will disagree with me on this, but I prefer to delay starting doubles until a dog is steady, force-broken, and sitting at heel to deliver. An unsteady dog will not even see the second fall unless the handler uses some sort of physical restraint. A dog that is not force-broken and that does not sit at heel to deliver will have all sorts of problems getting oriented at the line for the second retrieve. A hassle then will cause the dog to forget all about the bird that is still out there.

Duffy, when he was a very young dog, taught me about some of this. He was steady when I started him on doubles, but he was not yet force-broken, and his manner of delivery was to run into me full tilt and shove the bird into my midsection. I started him on doubles on bare ground, of course, and he quickly figured out a new way to handle them. He was so eager to get to the second bird that he would return only to within about 10 feet of me with the first one. There he would throw the bird to me and head for the other one. He was amazingly accurate with his tosses; I never had to move a step to field one of them (he would have made a great second baseman). Still, I quickly realized that he was not yet ready for doubles, so I stopped them until after I had force-broken him and had him sitting at heel to deliver. If I hadn't, he would have gradually returned less and less close to me with the first bird until he would be trying to bring them both in at once. I didn't need that problem, and neither do you.

Two different skills are required to complete a double. First, the dog must remember both falls long enough to find them one at a time. Second, the dog must not switch—that is, he must not wander from the area of one fall to the other. He must go to one area and stay there until he finds that bird. Then he must return to his handler with it. After that, he must go to the area of the second fall and stay there until he finds that bird. If he goes to one area and then leaves it to go to the other area, he has switched. This is a serious error for a retriever. In fact, it is an automatic disqualification in field trials. Why is switching so seriously penalized? Because the dog that switches will seldom find both birds and frequently will not find either one. The dog is really lost and is just wandering around trying to stumble on a bird. Such a dog will also disturb a lot of cover unnecessarily.

These two different skills, remembering both falls and retrieving without switching, should be taught separately. First, the dog should be taught to remember both falls in a manner that will not allow him to switch. Some sort of obstacle should be placed between the two falls—a fence, a row of bushes, a small building, anything that will keep the dog from switching. You can even start out at one corner of your house, tossing a bird along each of two adjacent sides. Naturally, this initial training in doubles should be done on bare ground so that the dog can see both birds from the line. Once you know he is getting the idea that there can be more than one bird to retrieve, you can move into light cover, but keep some sort of obstacle between the two falls for some time. Once he has formed the habit of making each retrieve individually, with no thought of switching from one bird to the other under these controlled conditions, you can eliminate the barriers. Until you have completed the switchproofing (see below), however, keep the falls widespread, at least 120 degrees apart. The purpose of all this is to build the dog's confidence. During the initial stages of learning about doubles, he should not experience many failures, nor should he be corrected often. The only way to ensure success is to make the work so simple that the dog cannot often fail. He will begin to enjoy rather than dread doubles. He would dislike them if he felt rushed, made numerous mistakes, and incurred many corrections.

When he is doing good work on widespread doubles in light cover out to your maximum length, whatever that is, you should start tempting him to switch. Shorten distances, move the falls closer together, and use short, dense cover (to make the bird more difficult to find). All dogs will switch if they are not trained to avoid it. Consequently, until you have switchproofed your dog, you will never be able to depend on him. Some dogs are more inclined to switch than others, but all dogs will do it until trained not to.

Your dog can switch in three ways, but the cure for each is the same. He might go to the area of the fall to which you sent him, search for the bird awhile, then give up and go to the area of the other fall. This can happen on either bird, the only difference being that if the dog does this on the memory bird after he has already picked up the diversion, there will be no bird in the area to which he switches. If he switches like this from the diversion to the memory bird, however, the memory-bird gun must beat him to the bird. The dog should never be allowed to pick up a bird after he has switched, so the gun should pick the bird up before the dog gets to it. If the dog switches from the memory bird to the diversion, after having already retrieved the diversion, there will be no bird for him to pick up, of course, so the gun can just stay in place. It is very important that guns do nothing to intimidate the dog if they have to pick up the bird, for the dog can become so fearful of the guns that he will refuse to retrieve at all. You will do all the correcting. The guns must leave the dog alone.

Another form of switching occurs when your dog forgets the memory bird and returns to the diversion area when sent for the memory bird. This kind of switch may indicate that he is not yet ready for switchproofing. The dog's memory for two falls should be very good before you start this training. Of course, every dog will do this occasionally, but if it happens very often, you might be rushing your dog too much. He will progress much more rapidly if you will take a step backward and develop his memory as described above before continuing with switchproofing.

I realize that there are disagreements among judges about which of these is a "true" switch and which is just "out of the area of the fall." For training purposes, however, they are different forms of the same problem, so I will call them all switches and skip the hair-splitting. The dog that does any of them will probably not complete the test, so the only disagreement is over why the dog is dropped from competition—for a switch or for a failure.

Now let's discuss your part in this training. Your objective is to take advantage of your dog's "place consciousness" as it relates to correction. Dogs will, for a time, avoid places in which they have been firmly corrected. Therefore, if you correct your dog in a place you don't want him to go to, he will avoid that location for a short time in the future. The more severe the correction, the longer the dog will avoid the area in which it took place.

In switchproofing, which places do you want him to avoid? The area of the fall to which he is switching, of course. That is where you should correct him. You first make sure that he doesn't get a bird there, by having the gun remove the bird before the dog reaches it. Then you run out there and correct the dog in that area. If you have to chase him all over the pasture—as I have done with every dog I ever trained—so be it. Drag him back to the area of the fall and correct him there.

Do not yell at your dog as soon as he starts to switch. Let him get all the way to the area he should be avoiding, and correct him there. If he starts to the diversion area from the line when you send him for the memory bird, don't say a thing to him. Let him get all the way there and then lower the boom. If you yell at him while he is running to the area, he will not be sure what you are correcting him for. He may be reluctant to leave your side the next time you say "Back."

How should you correct your dog? That depends on you and on your dog. When I was younger, I used to pick a dog up by the loose hide on his back and shake him while I spoke roughly to him. Now that is a lot of work for my tired old body, so I use a light whip for all but the most sensitive dogs. I select a whip that doesn't sting me too much when I hit myself on the back with it while wearing a T-shirt and regular shirt. I hit a dog only two or three times with the whip; any strokes beyond that do nothing for the dog but demonstrate that the trainer is out of control. Some dogs never need anything beyond scolding. Simply grab the dog's muzzle, look him in the eyes, and say something like "What are you trying to do, huh?" You have to understand your dog, and yourself, well enough to know how to correct him for switching.

It is important not to overdo any one correction. Switchproofing is a delicate operation, and it takes time. You will not accomplish it in one or two severe lessons. You will have to chip away at it patiently for some time and mix in plenty of confidence-building devices—widespread doubles and even singles, for instance—all through the process. If you overdo the correction for any one switch, you will intimidate your dog so that he will not return to the area for a normal retrieve such as a rerun of the same test. In fact, his performance on a rerun is a good gauge of how he is responding to the correction you are giving him. If he refuses to return to the area for a normal retrieve, you are being too heavy-handed. If he continues to switch to that area, you are not being severe enough.

You should use as many different areas as possible for switchproofing. That way your dog will not come to associate correction with a single spot or a few spots in your training grounds. He should come to associate correction with the act of switching, not with any geographic location. You use his place consciousness to do this, but if you do not change locations frequently, your dog may get the wrong message. You may simply be training him to stay away from a few well-known spots where he is always corrected.

The three R's of retriever training—rerun, rerun, rerun—are even more important in double marked retrieves than in singles. Reruns improve the dog's marking and memory by giving him another look at the falls from the line after he has made all the retrieves and knows where the birds are falling. Sometimes it is a good idea to start out a new double by giving the dog the memory bird as a single before running the complete double. This form of rerun is very useful for introducing a dog to more advanced work.

Naturally, you should not overdo reruns in any one training session. If your dog becomes too tired, he will not learn much, so let him rest while you work another dog or two. In half an hour your dog should be ready to go again. If he is still too tired, wait until the next training session.

These few training tips do not, of course, constitute a complete program for you and your dog in double marked retrieves. The intent here has been to explore some problems that have not been adequately covered in other books and to offer a few fresh approaches to dealing with those problems.

Figure 22.   Duck hunting on a rainy day. Two young hunters with some birds that they shot and that their golden retrieved for them.

Handling Techniques

HUNTING SITUATIONS

Double mark opportunities are not uncommon in duck hunting over decoys. For this reason, the dog must be placed where he can see the falls, and he must stay there until sent to retrieve, as has been mentioned earlier.

You will get an occasional double in jump shooting, too, so your dog must remain at heel not only until you shoot but also until you send him to retrieve. If he breaks for the first bird down, he will probably not see the second one. Here I am speaking of jump shooting while walking along a stream. If you do your jump shooting from a boat, you need to keep your dog from "jumping ship" too soon.

Doubles on pheasants are rare; at least they have been for me. Since this is the case and since pheasants are such capable athletes, I prefer to let my retrievers break to flush. Consequently, when I do get a double, my dog will not see the second bird. I handle this by "hot pursuit." While my dog is after the first pheasant, I take off after the second one. If my dog brings me his bird before I find the second one, I take it from him and tell him to "Hunt 'em out" in the area of the second fall. He will normally pick up the trail quickly and run the bird down. This is not classical hunting technique, but it works, and I am happy with it.

Once while dove hunting, I shot a bird that fell in a small patch of heavy cover. I searched for some time without finding it. Duffy was some distance away with my two sons. After a while I called to them to release Duffy so that he could come to help me. I blew the come-in whistle, and he headed my way. As he came, I continued looking for the downed dove. When Duffy arrived, I just mumbled "Hunt 'em out" and kept on searching. Duffy fell in behind me and followed me around instead of hunting as he normally would have. I said "Hunt 'em out!" a litle more firmly, still without looking at him. He continued to follow along behind me. Duffy has never been cover shy, so this surprised me. In fact, it infuriated me, and I turned to correct him, but when I finally took a good look at him, I saw that he had the dove in his mouth and was following me in an attempt to deliver it to me. He had found it immediately and had been very patient in his efforts to let me know it. It's a good thing dogs cannot talk—the tales they could tell about human folly!

Doubles on quail are fairly common, even for a miserable shot like me. Unless your dog is steady to wing and shot, however, you should not use him on quail. They fly too low and in too many directions. An unsteady dog will force you to pass up a lot of shots. Since I want my retrievers to break on pheasants, I really can't use them on quail. I much prefer to hunt quail over a pointing dog anyhow. I don't believe there is such a thing as an all-'round hunting dog. A jack-of-all-trades will be a master of none and not even passable at some. It would be possible to use a retriever on quail if you kept him at heel and used him only to fetch downed birds, but have you ever tried to heel a big dog through heavy quail cover all day? What a job.

FIELD TRIAL HANDLING

As in handling on single marks, it is very important in double marks to heel your dog to the line along a path that allows him to locate all the guns *before* he reaches the line. A professional trainer once told me that there is always such a path and that the handler has the right of way there. If anyone, even a judge, gets in the way, the handler should just walk right over him. The pro didn't completely convince me of all that, especially the part about walking over people, but I have found myself saying, "Uh, excuse me, sir (ma'am)" to a human obstacle on occasion.

Positioning your dog at the line is more complex in double marks than in singles, where you just point him at the guns. In doubles you want to be sure that he gets a good look at the memory bird, since he will have to remember it for a while before he retrieves it. This calls for judgment.

If the memory bird is in a really difficult spot, you should probably sit your dog facing it directly, especially if the diversion is an easy mark. If both are difficult, you will probably want to have the dog face a spot between the two marks but favoring the memory bird. Never, never place him so that he faces the diversion, even if it appears to be much the more difficult fall to mark. Keep in mind the fact that your dog has to remember the memory bird longer.

When the diversion is a short, easy shot flier (live bird), some handlers try to prevent their dogs from even seeing the guns for it until the memory bird has hit the ground. This may sound unusual, but there are reasons for it. A shot flier is much more exciting for the dog than the control (thrown dead) memory bird. It doesn't take dogs long to figure out that three people and a stack of bird crates in one location mean there will be a shot flier and that two people with no bird crates indicate a control bird. Once a dog figures that out, he will want to concentrate on the shot flier rather than on the memory bird when he comes to the line for a double with a control bird for the memory bird and a shot flier for the diversion. Some handlers try to prevent this by keeping their dogs from seeing the shot flier guns until after the memory bird has been thrown. This allows the dog to concentrate on the memory bird. There is no way he will fail to see the flier, since it will flap its wings, squawk, and be brought down with two to four shotgun blasts. The dog will see the flier. The only problem is that he may be so surprised by the live bird that he will break. That is the risk these handlers are taking, and perhaps they are wise to take it for the sake of the dogs. You will have to decide for yourself whether it is better to let your dog see the diversion guns in this test and risk having him not really watch the memory bird, or to prevent him from seeing the guns and risk a break. Decisions like this are part of what makes field trialing so much fun, if frustrating at times. No matter which way you go, your dog may run into problems, and there will be several gallery quarterbacks all too eager to tell you that you should have done it the other way. Make your own decision based on your knowledge of your dog, and you'll be right more often than not. Enjoy the times it works out right, accept the times it doesn't, and ignore the gallery quarterbacks.

Knowing when to send your dog to each mark is important. As soon as both birds are down, many dogs will swing their heads back from the diversion to the memory bird. If yours does this, do not send him for the diversion until he has swung his head back to it and locked in on it. Encourage him to look at the diversion by patting your leg and using your hand to line the dog, but never send him for the memory bird first. If you do, he will almost certainly switch and be eliminated from the stake. Instead, get him to come back to the diversion and then send him. That's the bird he should retrieve first.

As he returns to you with the diversion bird, turn your body so that you are facing the memory bird. That way, when your dog sits at your left side, to deliver, he will be facing his next retrieve, and you will have less difficulty lining up correctly than you would have if you were still facing the diversion.

Take the bird from him as described in Chapter 1, and put it behind your hip on the side opposite your dog. That way it will not distract him from his next retrieve. Do not try to give the bird to the judge or lay it on the ground. Just hold it behind you until your dog is off and running after the memory bird. Then you can hold it out behind you for the judge to take.

While your dog is still sitting at heel after he has delivered the diversion, give him a second or two to reorient himself before you send him after the memory bird. Let him reestablish his mark. You will be able to tell when he has done this by the intensity of his gaze at the area of the fall. When he really has it located again, send him—but not before.

What I am describing here is the way you can help your dog most between birds on doubles. You will see some strange handling techniques, especially in fun trials. Sometimes they work, too, but don't be misled by them. If you are going to imitate anyone, pick the most successful pro in your area, not some clumsy beginner who happens to have a dog that works well in spite of the

Figure 23.   Sending the dog for the memory bird. Notice that the handler has put the first bird behind his hip on the side away from the dog.

handler's errors. I once saw a handler allow his dog to sit facing behind him after the dog returned with the first bird. He took the bird with his left hand and then waved his right hand over his head and said "Back!" Although the dog couldn't even see the handler's right arm from where he was sitting, he whirled around and made the other retrieve very well. It was an extremely simple test. I doubt if the dog could have managed a really tough one with that kind of handling.

There are several schools of thought about when to give your dog a little hand signal as you send him to retrieve. Here I am speaking of placing your left hand (assuming your dog is sitting at your left side) by your dog's head as you say "Back!" Some handlers do this every time they send their dogs. Others do it only on blind retrieves, reasoning that the dog should know where the marks are. Still others use the hand on blinds and on all marks except the diversion bird. All of these approaches seem to work with most dogs, but an occasional dog is bothered by the hand.

Mickey, a golden I trained years ago, was such a dog. If the hand didn't get down there soon enough, he would look up at me, thereby losing his concentration on the mark. This became a progressively worse problem in that he looked up sooner and sooner until finally he didn't even wait until the bird hit the ground—and his marking fell apart. I went back to square one with him, only this time I didn't use the hand signal at all; I just sent him with the voice command "Back!" This seemed to solve the problem. He never looked up at me when I didn't say "Back!" soon enough to suit him. Later on, if he was a little confused on a mark, I could use my hand to settle him down, but that was all I used it for, except on blind retrieves, of course.

Ever since Mickey, I have been inclined to reserve the use of the hand for blind retrieves and for those marking situations in which the dog seems somewhat confused. If he needs the hand signal on a mark, I give it to him; otherwise, I use only the voice command. Perhaps I have overreacted to one dog's idiosyncrasy, but it has worked well for me. Others use the hand signal for every mark and have no problem. Still others feel that the hand will interfere with the dog's mark on the diversion bird but will help on the memory bird. You will have to figure out what works best for you and your dog.

Whatever else you do or don't do with your left hand, never slap your dog with it when he fails to look where you want him to. You will see inexperienced or ill-tempered trainers do this, espe-

Figure 24. A young golden approaches a shackled mallard.

cially on blinds. It is totally counterproductive. You want the dog to trust that left hand, to believe in it, not to wonder if it is going to smack him up the side of the head. If you feel that your dog must be corrected, try some other method. Let him feel reassured when you put your hand down beside his head. The hand has to be there to help him; it will be a serious distraction if he fears it.

Again, as you leave the line after the test, thank the judges and depart rapidly.

Training Tests

The rest of this chapter is devoted to diagrams and explanations for double marked retrieve training tests. These tests show how the relative positions of the two marks create complications for the dogs. Cover, terrain, and wind conditions were discussed in Chapter 1, "Single Marked Retrieves." Since each mark in a double is really a single mark in itself, what was said about these factors in Chapter 1 applies equally here. Cover, terrain, and wind will be discussed here only in those instances in which they create a special problem in a double that was not covered in Chapter 1.

Doubles are seen often in the derby stake, frequently in the qualifying stake, and sometimes in the amateur and open stakes at field trials. More often than not in the all-age stakes (qualifying, amateur, and open), a blind retrieve will be associated with the double mark. Mixed blinds and marks are covered in the chapter on suction blinds. As you go over the diagrams in this chapter, however, it is well to remember that a blind—or multiple blinds—can be mixed in with any of the tests.

Derby stakes do not have blind retrieve requirements, but I have seen several derby dogs fail to see the memory bird in a double and then pick it up by being lined to it, just as in a blind retrieve. This is perfectly legal, although a dog that requires any handling after the initial lining will be penalized. How severe the penalty is will depend on the individual judges and on how many other dogs are being handled to the memory bird.

Double retrieves in all-age stakes are typically longer and tighter than those in the derby. All-age dogs are expected to do more difficult work than that required of the younger dogs. Some judges, however, set up very demanding doubles for the derby dogs to run, and at least some of the dogs get through them at every trial.

THROWING PATTERNS FOR DOUBLE MARKS

Figure 25 illustrates the four patterns for throwing double marks. Every double you will ever see is based on one of these. The sequence of the throws can be varied; the distance of each throw can be lengthened or shortened; the angle between the falls can be loosened or tightened; and all manner of cover, terrain, and wind combinations can be introduced. In spite of such variations, however, every double will make use of one of these throwing patterns. It is important that your dog have plenty of experience with each of them.

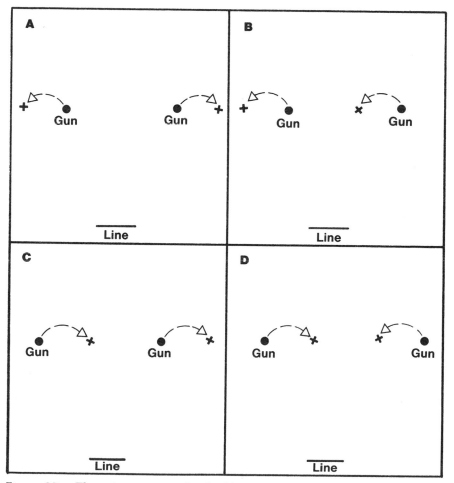

Figure 25. Throwing patterns for double marks.

In pattern 25–A both birds are thrown outward—away from each other. Either bird may be thrown first. (Remember that the first bird thrown is normally the last bird retrieved and is therefore called the memory bird.) Generally speaking, this outward pattern offers the dog the least temptation to switch. With a good, wide angle between the falls, this is a good pattern for a dog's initial doubles.

Patterns B and C are opposites: in B, both birds are thrown to the handler's left, and in C, both are thrown to the handler's right. In either pattern the test is typically more difficult if the memory bird falls between the two guns. If the test is set up this way, the dog with too much exposure to the type-A pattern (both birds thrown outward) will tend to search on the wrong side of the gun for the memory bird; the dog will hesitate to go between the guns.

In pattern 25–D both birds are thrown inward (between the guns). This offers the dog the maximum temptation to switch. In all the other patterns, at least one of the guns acts as a sort of barrier between the two falls. In pattern 25–D no such barrier exists. This is a good pattern to use when you are serious about training your dog not to switch; it is a bad one to use when your dog is just starting to learn doubles.

In all marking tests it is very important that the guns continue to face in the direction of the birds they have just thrown. Dogs will tend to use the direction the gun faces as a clue to the placement of the memory bird. If the gun turns around after throwing the bird, the dog will be misled. This is really not fair to the dog. When you act as a gun for someone else's dog, be sure to stand facing the bird you have thrown until the dog has picked it up. Request that others do the same for your dog.

Length (distance) considerations for doubles are somewhat more complex than they are for singles. Of course, the length of the tests you give your dog still depends on your personal goals, the dog's experience level, and the visibility factors (these considerations apply for all retriever training). In doubles, however, another factor applies, and that is the distance between the falls. The shorter this distance is, the more the length (between the line and the fall) affects the difficulty of the test. In setting up long, tight marks, you should be sure that the areas of the two falls are adequately distinct. If you don't do this, how will you know when to correct your dog for switching?

The area of a fall is difficult to define. Most of us learn unconsciously to recognize it as we go along in retriever training. Someone once told me that, as a rough estimate, the area of a fall could be defined as an area around the fall with a diameter that is one-fifth of the distance from the line to the fall. That is just a good rough estimate, of course. Other factors must be considered. For example, the area of the fall for the memory bird should be larger than that for the diversion. Also, a dog may be expected to hunt a larger area in very light cover than in heavy cover, and so on.

The important thing to remember is that in all multiple marking tests the areas of the separate falls should be adequately distinct so that you can reasonably correct your dog for switching.

LONG MEMORY BIRD

A popular test, especially for inexperienced dogs, is the one illustrated in Figure 26, in which the memory bird is substantially farther from the line than the diversion is. Any of the four throwing patterns shown in Figure 25 can be used, of course, although the diagram shows the outward pattern. The length of the throws should depend on the skill of the dog being trained; so should the distance between the falls.

In this test, the dog will usually be able to pick up the short diversion bird very quickly. For this reason, his memory is not severely tested by time; he does not have to remember the other bird very long, as he would if the diversion were longer or required a long hunt.

The only problem this test presents is that some inexperienced dogs will be reluctant to go so far for the memory bird after picking up the diversion near or relatively near the line. If your dog has this problem, run him on the memory bird as a single mark once or twice before you run the double. In fact, this is a good idea any time you introduce a new test to an inexperienced dog.

Normally this test should be run with a type-A wind (straight downwind). The type-B wind makes the test considerably more difficult in that, in seeking the memory bird, the dog is likely to drift behind the gun where he could be distracted by the bird sack. The type-C wind is totally unfair to the young dog because it blows scent from the bird sack of the diversion gun to the dog as he runs to the memory bird. This sort of thing is done in trials, even in the derby stake, but you should avoid it in training until your dog is being readied for competition. The distraction is too much for the inexperienced dog. You want to encourage a novice dog to use his nose, not ignore it.

You can use terrain and cover variations to stiffen this test up as your dog progresses. For example, if the test is run on the side

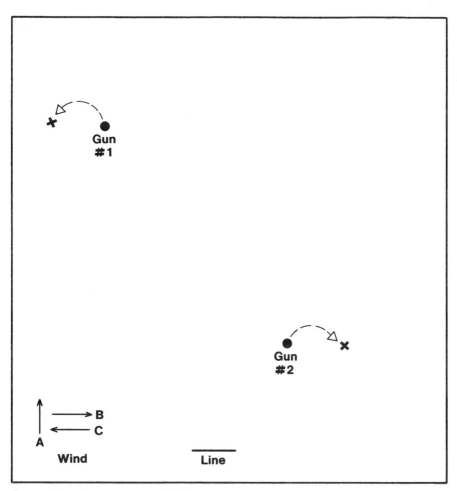

Figure 26. Long memory bird.

of a hill with the memory bird higher than the diversion—and with a type-A wind—it will really test whether your dog can mark. Also, if the diversion is thrown into very tough cover, your dog may have a long hunt there, thus putting a time test on his memory as far as his search for the memory bird is concerned.

This test can also be run in the water, with both birds on land, both in the water, or one on land and the other in the water (either way).

As you can see, this is a very versatile test, one you can use as long as you are training your dog. If you really want to toughen it up, on land or in water, make the diversion a shot flier. This makes the dog less inclined to watch the memory bird all the way to the ground or into the water. Dogs tend to become very excited about shot fliers, and they learn quickly that the presence of two human beings with shotguns in addition to a thrower at one place usually means that a flier will be used. Dogs cannot concentrate as well on the memory bird when the diversion is a flier.

FIFTY-FIFTY

Figure 27 illustrates a basic double mark in which both birds fall about the same distance from the line. The "both out" throwing pattern is used in the figure, because the other throwing patterns present special cases that will be covered separately.

In the illustration, the memory bird is on the left. Actually, you should vary this often enough so that your dog does not come to expect either bird always to be thrown first.

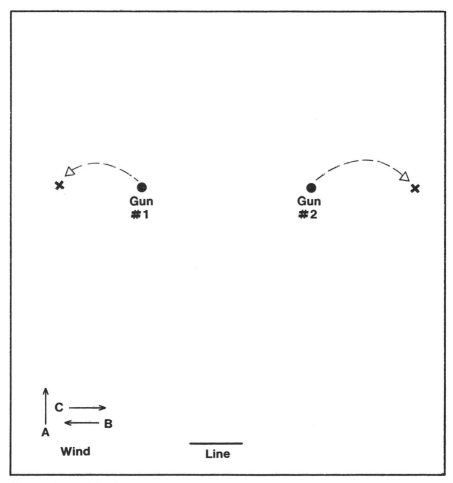

Figure 27.   Fifty-fifty.

When you start your dog on doubles, possibly even in the bare-ground days, you will use this test often. Once he is familiar with doubles from the short-diversion–long-memory-bird test, this one offers a natural way to extend the dog's memory. In the early days, the distance between the falls should be wide, the marks short, and the cover light. You will find the trial-and-success technique more effective than the trial-and-error method, which is likely to overtax the dog. No dog—and no human being—can remain enthusiastic about anything at which he fails most of the time. Isn't that true in your own experience? No one enjoys being wrong all the time.

The advantage of this test is that it tests your dog's memory. He can no longer pick up the diversion quickly and easily. It is about as difficult to find as the memory bird, so the dog may have to hunt carefully to find it.

As the dog progresses, you can increase the difficulty of this test by making the angle (from memory bird to line to diversion) more acute, by lengthening the distance between the line and the falls, and by adding terrain and cover complications. You can also use this test in water.

Generally this test should be run with the type-A wind (straight downwind). The type-B wind actually simplifies the search for the memory bird by encouraging the dog to drift to the left (away from the diversion and any temptation to switch). The type-C wind makes the test tougher, for the dog is inclined to drift behind the gun on the memory bird and be distracted by the bird sack or be tempted to switch.

This is another ideal situation in which to use a shot flier as the diversion bird. A dog may have trouble concentrating on the memory bird under such conditions. In training, you can improve your dog's concentration by setting up this test with one control bird and one shot flier, and then running the control bird as a single, using no double at all. The dog will decide that maybe all those shotguns and throwers and bird crates out there at the diversion position don't mean a thing sometimes. After a few such exercises he will pay closer attention to the memory bird, because it may be the only bird he gets. This is a good way to cure head-swinging of any kind.

THE HIP POCKET

In Figure 28 we have a type of double that can be made either very easy or extremely difficult, depending on the distance from the falls to the line and the distance between the two falls. If

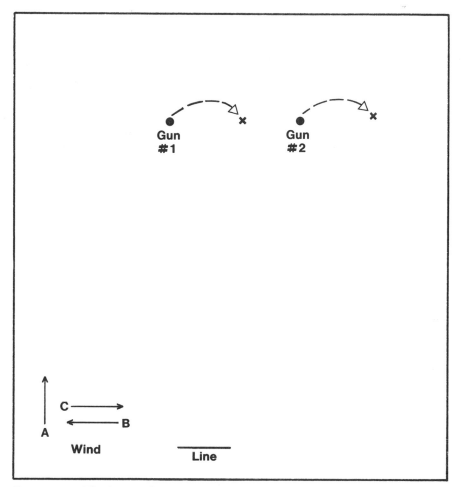

Figure 28. The hip pocket.

the falls are widely spaced and close to the line, the test will be easy. The longer and tighter the throws are, the tougher the test becomes. At a certain point—when the falls are very close to-gether—it starts to appear as if the memory bird is thrown into the hip pocket of the diversion gun.

When the test is short and wide, you can use any of the three winds shown, and your dog should be able to complete the re-trieves. When the test is long and wide, the type-C wind is not so bad, and the type-B wind offers the usual confusion factor from the bird sack. The type-A wind is, of course, preferred. When the test is long and tight, the only reasonable wind is type A. This form of the test is tough enough without squirrelly winds to com-plicate it!

In its long and tight version this is a test for the more experi-enced dog, not something for young derby dogs, no matter what the wind conditions. The temptation to switch is just too much for the young dogs. As a matter of fact, even the old campaigners will very often want to switch on this one. The difference is that they can be handled out of trouble, whereas the derby dog usually cannot.

The point of all this is that you should not make this test any tougher than your dog can handle at any point in his development. Until he is more experienced and handling very well, don't make this one too long or too tight.

As long as you keep it within your dog's capabilities, you can use a shot flier as the diversion bird in this test. You can also use this test in water as well as on land. In water, be very sure that your dog will not be tempted to switch beyond his current capabilities, however, for you will find it difficult to correct him in the water.

THE SWITCHEROO

A very popular switching test appears in Figure 29. With both birds thrown inward (toward each other), the dog will be more tempted to switch than with any of the other throwing patterns. In all the other ones the guns act as a sort of barrier. Here, however, there is nothing between the falls.

Naturally, the closer together the marks are the more severe is the temptation to switch. Similarly, the farther the falls are from the line, the greater the temptation.

Terrain can be used to make this test more difficult. If, for example, it is set up on the side of a hill with the memory bird above the diversion, many dogs will drift downhill into trouble when they go after the memory bird. If a ditch or patch of heavy cover stretches between the line and the falls, the dogs will have trouble reorienting themselves when they get to the other side of the cover on each mark. This could cause some switching. The type-A wind is preferred if the falls are at all close together. The type-B wind, if it is not a gale, isn't too bad, for it tends to keep the dog in the area of the memory bird, and most switches will take place from that area. The dogs will find the diversion and then switch after a long hunt for the memory bird. A strong type-B wind, however, could cause some dogs to drift into the memory bird area while going to or hunting the diversion area; this wind could also blow the dogs behind the memory-bird gun, where bird-sack scent could cause a problem.

The type-C is really too difficult for all but fully trained licensed trial dogs. It encourages the dog to switch from the memory bird area.

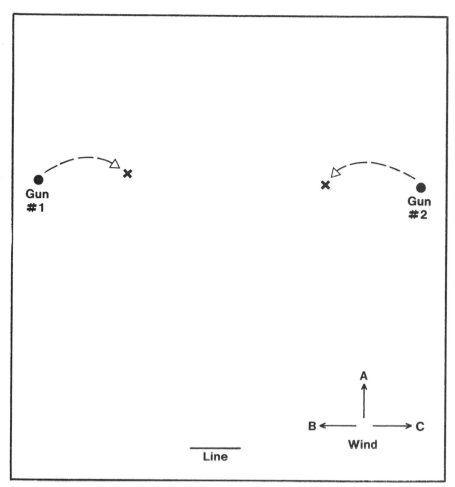

Figure 29. The switcheroo.

If the falls are at all tight (close together), stick with the type-A wind. The placement of the falls makes this test tough enough without any additional complication from crosswinds.

The switcheroo can be used in water as well as on land. Do not give your dog any switching tests in water until he is thoroughly switchproofed on land, however. You simply cannot get to him to correct him as you should when he is in the water. All water training should lag behind the corresponding land work, of course, but this is especially true of switchproofing.

SHORT MEMORY BIRD

Figure 30 illustrates a variation on the hip pocket double shown in Figure 28. In this pattern the memory bird is considerably closer to the line than the diversion is. This may seem like a

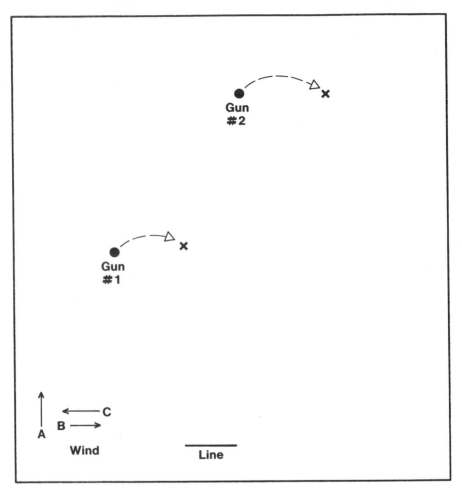

Figure 30. Short memory bird.

simpler test than the regular hip pocket, but it is actually considerably tougher for most dogs.

The typical dog will overrun the memory bird in this test. The
reason for this is that in all too many exercises the memory bird is
as far or farther from the line than the diversion is. The dog forms
the habit of running at least as far as the diversion with his
"hunting switch" turned off before he gets serious about looking
for the memory bird. I have actually seen a dog run right past a big
red plastic dummy on bare ground three times before he got the
idea of this test! (The dog was mine, as a matter of fact.)

Bare ground and white dummies are definitely in order for
introducing this test to your dog. Let him learn that a short memory bird is possible before you make the exercise very difficult.
Keep in mind that the dog will learn much more from success
than he will from failure.

It is best to use a type-A wind (straight downwind) for this test. The type-B wind will blow scent from the memory bird to the dog as he goes to the diversion. If this causes him to turn and pick up the memory bird first, he will very likely not complete the test, because when he is sent back out for the diversion, he will think that he has already picked it up and will return to the area of the memory bird. That is a switch. The type-C wind is a little better, but it can get the dog into bird-sack trouble on both birds. This test is plenty tough enough without any little added wrinkles like that. Use the type-A wind and you will give your dog all the challenge he needs.

While it doesn't need added complications, this test can be made into an all-age double by running it so that both marks are thrown uphill, or both downhill.

This test can also be run in the water.

THE FOUNTAIN

The test shown in Figure 31 takes its name from the fact that, from the line, the birds look as if they are coming out of a common source (a fountain) and going in opposite directions.

The first step in running this test is to help your dog see that there are two sets of guns out there. If a flier is used for the diversion, this problem is intensified considerably, for most dogs tend to focus on a flier in any test. Be sure that your dog sees both guns before you call for the birds, even if this takes a few minutes of heeling around the area. He will never complete the test if he doesn't see both guns before he starts, but will probably return to the diversion area when sent for the memory bird—and there he is finished (a switch).

The type-A wind is probably the best to use most of the time. The type-C wind may blow scent from the bird sack near the diversion gun to the dog as he goes out to the memory bird. This is unfair to a young dog, although it is done in licensed trial competition (where dogs are expected to be able to cope with this kind of distraction on their way to a marked or even a blind retrieve). The type-B wind will tend to blow the dog behind the memory-bird gun. This, too, is done in licensed trials, but don't pull it on a young dog. This test is difficult enough without such a complication. When your dog is ready for something more challenging than straight downwind, you will know it.

Terrain can also be used to make this test more difficult for the experienced dog. Throwing the memory bird uphill and the

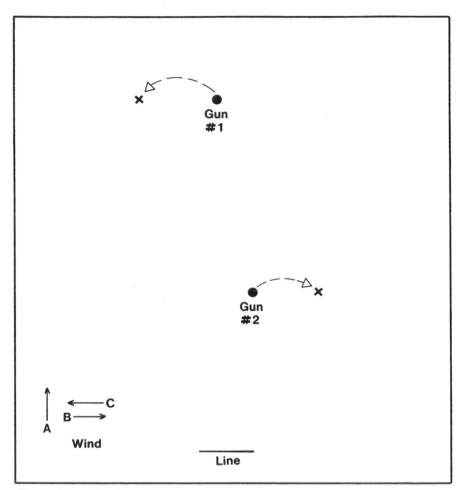

Figure 31. The fountain.

diversion downhill makes the test much more difficult; dogs will tend to drift downhill on the memory bird and get lost.

This is a very good water test also—for the dog that can handle it well on land.

SADISTIC SWITCHEROO

The test shown in Figure 32 is an extremely difficult variation of the switcheroo. Here the memory bird is closer to the line than the diversion is, making this another short memory bird test, and a very tough one at that. In setting this one up, take care to keep the falls far enough apart so that the test doesn't become an in-line (or over-under) double. That is really a trick test, in that the dog is expected to run through the area of one fall, full of

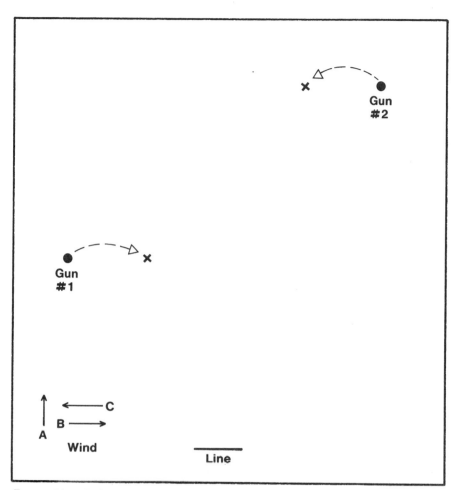

Figure 32. Sadistic switcheroo.

scent, when going after the other bird. That test can be done in water, where the scent problem doesn't exist, but it is an unreasonable test on land.

The problem in the sadistic switcheroo is that the dog will run too deep on the memory bird because it is so much closer to the line than the diversion is. Once he has run past the memory bird, he is very near the area of the diversion bird. Many dogs cannot resist the temptation to switch under these conditions.

The type-A wind (straight downwind) is the best one to use. The type-B wind will blow scent from the memory bird to the dog as he goes after the diversion. If the dog turns and picks up the memory bird then, he will never get the diversion, for he will think that he has already picked it up. He will switch back to the area of the memory bird again. He could get lucky, of course, and drive too deep, wind up in the diversion area, and get it that way. However, he would then be succeeding by doing everything wrong; that is no way to train a dog. The type-C wind is a friendly wind, unless the dog drives too deep on the memory bird; then the wind will pull him right back into the diversion area. For this reason the type-C wind is probably the one most frequently used in licensed trials on this test. It helps the dogs that do it right and hinders the dogs that fall into the trap.

If the memory bird is on higher ground than the diversion, the test will be that much harder, because the dog will tend to drift downhill toward the diversion as he goes after the memory bird.

Dense cover around the memory bird is very friendly, for it will tend to slow the dog down and induce him to hunt the area instead of driving on through.

DETOURING DOUBLE

Figure 33 presents a double land mark designed to penalize the dog that does not take clean, straight lines to the falls. This test is especially difficult for the dog that avoids cover. The line is positioned on a knoll. The memory bird is thrown on another knoll on the other side of a draw full of dense cover. The diversion bird is thrown out on the flat in light cover.

Most dogs will have little trouble with the diversion. The memory bird is also quite easy if the dog takes a straight line through the dense cover. For such a dog, this test should go fast.

The dog that tries to run around the cover, however, will face serious problems. To run around the cover means to run toward the diversion bird for many yards before reaching the end of the cover patch. Most young dogs will not make the turn and go to the memory bird after running some distance toward the other fall. They will keep right on going straight, and that will constitute a switch in this test. If the diversion is a shot flier, this tendency to continue running toward it will be intensified.

In training your dog to take straight lines to marks like this, it is necessary in this test to set up the memory bird as a single. If your dog tries to run around the cover, correct him when he reaches the end of the cover patch—at about the point where he turns to go up the knoll for the mark. That will make him want to avoid that place on the rerun. The only way he can avoid that place is to run through the cover patch. Do this with a lot of singles in a lot of places before you try him on this test as a double. You might

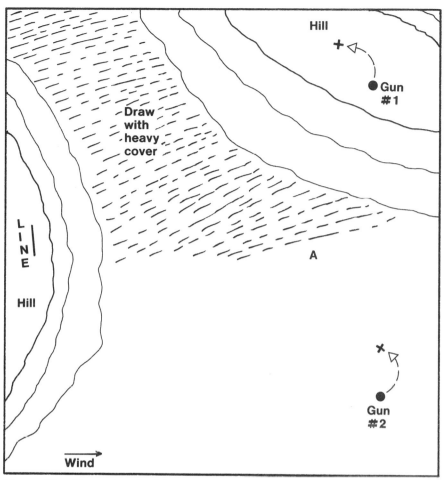

Figure 33.   Detouring double.

even give him this double on a rerun after the single when he
starts doing the single well.

   How do you correct your dog way out there at the end of the
cover patch? There are several techniques, but they are all so
complex that you should not try to learn them from a book. See
your professional trainer. The pro will teach you what to do and
what not to do and will watch you to be sure that you understand
the correction techniques.

   Do not correct your dog as soon as he starts to veer off around
the cover. That is likely to make him think that he is being corrected for leaving your side rather than for taking the wrong line
to the bird. Try to see the situation from the dog's point of view
and you'll understand why this is true. Once he thinks he is being
punished for leaving when you say "Back," you really have problems. Avoid them by never correcting your dog close to the line, no

matter how badly he performs. Let him move some distance from you before you correct him. As D. L. Walters says, "Let your dog get deep into a problem before you correct him." That is good advice from one of the top professional retriever trainers in the nation.

TWO WET ONES

In Figure 34 we have a double in which both throws land in the water. You should give your dog plenty of practice on these retrieves so that he expects to find the birds in water instead of al-

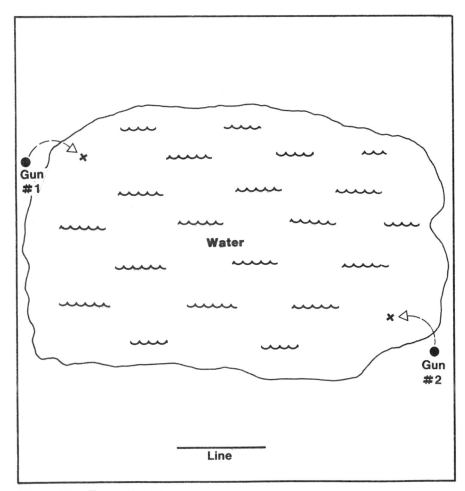

Figure 34. Two wet ones.

ways on land. Dogs that are given too many water marks on land across a stretch of water tend to become bank runners. Why not? There is never anything in the water to hold them there, so why shouldn't they get out of the water as quickly as possible and get in as seldom as possible? If you give your dog 80 percent of his water marks actually in the water, he will have no trouble with the other 20 percent. If you reverse those percentages, however, he will have all sorts of trouble with the 20 percent that are in the water.

Be certain, however, that the memory bird is not thrown so that it will drift while the dog retrieves the diversion. It is best to throw the memory bird into some cover in the water. In fact, throwing both marks into cover in water is a good idea whenever possible. If there is only one spot of cover, use it for the memory bird. Let the diversion fall into open water. That way, the dog will have no problem finding it. If the memory bird drifts, however, the dog can start to lose confidence in his marking ability. Confidence is too important a quality to risk losing.

MIXED DOUBLE

Figure 35 shows a water double in which the memory bird is thrown into a small patch of cover out in the water and the diversion is thrown on land across the pond. Ideally, the diversion in this test should be a shot flier.

Notice that there is a patch of cover in the water between the line and the diversion. To get that bird, the dog has to swim right through this cover and then leave the water. Because this is the diversion and especially because it is a flier, the dog will have no difficulty with it. Most dogs that are experienced with fliers become very excited when they see a flier setup—two guns and a thrower plus a bird crate or two. They know what that means, and it is difficult for them to concentrate on the memory bird, which is a control bird (a thrown dead bird).

In this test many dogs will pick up the diversion very quickly and then miss the memory bird altogether. They will land beyond it and hunt the shore and then go on up a nearby hill and hunt some more.

There are two reasons for this. First, the first bird they retrieved was on land on the other side of some cover in the water. Many dogs will look for the memory bird in the same kind of place; this tendency is intensified when the diversion is a flier, for the dogs tend to pay so much attention to the flier throughout the test

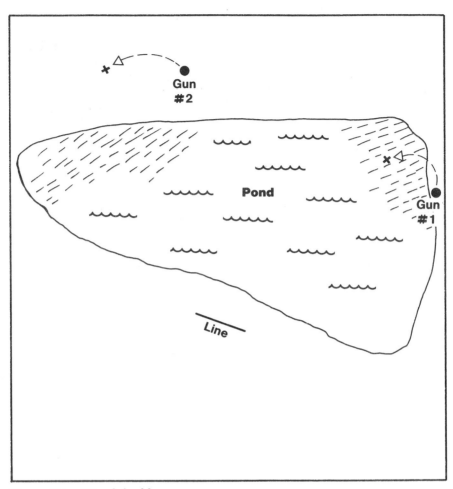

Figure 35. Mixed double.

that they never get a good mark on the memory bird. Such a dog will either get lucky and bump into the bird as he swims through the cover or will continue on to the land and hunt there.

The second reason why dogs miss the memory bird in this test is that many trainers seldom train on water tests in which the birds are actually thrown into the water. It is so much easier to throw them on land on the other side of the water. It is easier to find a suitable place, easier to position the guns, easier to pick up unretrieved birds, easier in every way. For this reason, many dogs are insufficiently trained to look for marks in cover in the water. On the rare occasions when they get this kind of work, they find both birds in the water instead of finding one on land and the

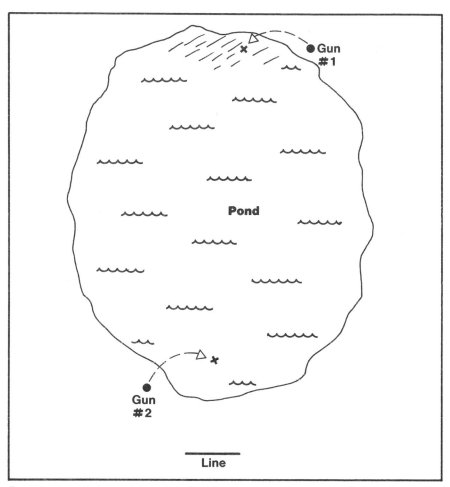

Figure 36. Over–under water double.

other in water. With many trainers, this is an all-or-nothing-at-all situation—usually nothing-at-all.

Every dog should be worked on marks in cover in the water frequently. It is not easy to find places suitable for this, but a search is worth the effort. Birds fall into cover in water during field trials, and they certainly fall there in hunting.

One more point must be made: every once in a while, have a mark thrown from a boat into a patch of cover in the middle of a pond. This will teach your dog that birds can land a long way from shore, not just around the edge of a body of water.

OVER–UNDER WATER DOUBLE

The pattern for an over–under, or in-line, double marked retrieve in water appears in Figure 36. This kind of exercise has long since been discarded in land tests, where the scent from the diversion bird distracts the dog as he goes to the memory bird. No such problem exists in water, however, so the test is still used there, at least occasionally. Actually, this pattern is most often used for the first and third bird in a triple.

The most important thing to know about this test is when *not* to use it. If your dog is still going through switchproofing and is still being corrected for returning to the wrong area, do not give this test. Here, the dog is required to go through a recently hunted area to get to the memory bird. What could be more confusing?

I have seen dogs at that stage of training absolutely refuse to leave the line when sent for the memory bird in this test—and who can blame them? They are still being corrected for doing this in various switching tests. Other dogs will detour around the problem, some even going by land all the way around the pond. That is not good, either.

It is best not to use this test with a dog that is not thoroughly switchproofed and into qualifying-stakes work (triples and blind retrieves). Even then, do not overdo it. All you want is for your dog to be sufficiently familiar with this setup so as not to be confused if it occurs in a field trial or during hunting.

Above all else *never* set up a test like this on land.

3. TRIPLE MARKED RETRIEVES

Training Tips

A triple marked retrieve, or triple mark, is a test in which three birds are thrown in three different places, and the dog is expected to retrieve the birds one at a time. Since this is a marking test, the dog is allowed to watch the birds being thrown. Dogs normally retrieve the last bird thrown first, so the last bird is called the diversion. Dogs will retrieve the other two in either possible sequence, so both of them are called memory birds.

A triple really tests the dog's memory. He has to remember the locations of the two memory birds while he finds the diversion, and then he has to remember the placement of one memory bird while he retrieves the other. If the falls are such that he has to hunt a long time for either of the first two, the dog will need considerable experience before he is even able to remember that there is still another bird out there somewhere.

Initially, triples should be introduced by running the dog on a double and then putting a simple third bird in on the rerun. Doing this on bare ground with big white dummies is a good idea, at least until the dog becomes used to the idea of retrieving three falls instead of two. Probably every new phase of retriever training can best be started on bare ground, but it is difficult to force ourselves to go back to bare ground once we have advanced into cover on a previous phase. If we would think in terms of how to get the idea across to the dog most quickly, however, we would not be inclined to regard bare ground as a regression.

Lengthen the falls out to whatever limits you have established before moving into cover, and then shorten up significantly when you do start working on triples in cover.

Figure 37.   A yellow Lab brings in a duck.

Triples require a greater degree of the two skills a dog needs for doubles: memory and switchproofing. Memory comes with experience, preferably trial-and-success experience. Switchproofing is the same in triples as it is in doubles, but you should not start a dog on triples until he has been thoroughly switchproofed on doubles. Even so, do not be surprised if he tries to switch a few times on triples anyhow. Whenever he does, look on it as an opportunity to get in a good correction. Don't let it irritate you. A complete job of switchproofing takes a long time.

The three R's—rerun, rerun, rerun—are important in triples, too. Both the dog's marking and his memory are improved by rerunning every test at least once, and more often if required. The danger of fatigue is greater in triples, however—especially in water triples—so be careful not to overwork your dog in any one training session. There is always tomorrow.

Some dogs tend to be head-swingers on multiple marks: they swing their heads away from one mark before it hits the ground to look for the next one. This happens on doubles as well as on triples. Naturally, a dog that does this will not be able to mark the falls as well as the dog that watches each bird all the way to the ground.

There are two parts to the cure for head-swinging. First, in training sessions, you should frequently set up for a double or a triple but have only one bird thrown. This is actually running a single off of a multiple mark setup. After doing enough of these, your dog will come to doubt that there will always be as many falls as there are guns out in the field. This will encourage him to concentrate on the first fall until he hears the gun go off for the second one. When running him on this type of test, don't send him for the single while he is looking at one of the other guns, which he probably will do at first. Instead, encourage him to swing his head back to the bird that was actually thrown before you send him. If he swings his head away from the throw and you send him then, he will fail the test more often than not—and learn nothing. The purpose of this training is to get him to stop swinging his head too soon, so it makes no sense to send him when he is looking the wrong way. I have seen people do this and rationalize it by saying, "That will teach the old rascal a lesson." Unfortunately, it doesn't. It only causes him to fail the test, and then he catches hell for that, too.

The second part of the cure for head-swinging is rotating your own body slightly away from one mark and toward the next when it is time for your dog to swing his head. You should turn slightly to face each fall just before it is thrown, and your dog should interpret your movement as a body signal. If you don't rotate a little, the dog will know that there will not be another fall—as in the setup where you give him a single off a multiple marking test. If you do rotate a little, he will come to know that there is to be another bird. Teaching a dog to read such a body signal takes time—and consistency on your part.

As you take your dog through this cure for head-swinging, you will notice that he has a stronger inclination to break as a result of not knowing how many falls to expect. If he has had a breaking problem before, it might be a good idea to put him back on the belt cord, or whatever device you used to steady him, for a while. That way you won't have to worry about two problems, head-swinging and breaking, during this training.

Many retrievers can never be completely cured of head-swinging. If you use these techniques whenever the problem comes up, however, you can keep head-swinging under control. Another method is to give your dog nothing but single marks for a day or two immediately before each field trial. This will stop head-swinging and improve marking for a short period—long enough to get through the trial.

By the time you are running triples, you will also be honoring another dog's work. A dog *honors* when he sits at heel near the line while another dog retrieves. It is a test of steadiness. This is required in the all-age stakes. An occasional triple is seen in the derby, where honoring is not required, but nevertheless you should be honoring by the time you are doing triples—at least in training. Actually, it is better to start honoring when your dog is doing good work on doubles.

To train for honoring, go back to singles on bare ground to spare the dog any difficulty in finding the dummy. Run your dog a time or two, just to take the edge off him, and then move to the honor position and have another handler come up to the line with a dog. Command "Stay" softly to your dog before the dummy is thrown. There is no reason to shout. Your dog will break when the other handler says "Back" anyway, and if you are loud, you will interfere with the working dog. Of course, you should have your dog under some kind of restraint so that you can control him when he breaks—and he will break at first. I use the belt cord for this.

When the other handler sends the working dog, yours will attempt to join in the retrieving effort; in other words, he will break. You should stop him with the belt cord, or whatever restraint you are using, and then *roughly* reposition him—*all without saying a word.* Any noise from you will only interfere with the working dog. Once your dog is back where he belongs, say "Stay" again, and say it softly.

Personally, I use the command "Stay" only for honoring— never for steadying. That way, when my dog hears "Stay," he knows that he will not retrieve anything that time, so he sits back and relaxes. If a person uses "Stay" to steady the working dog—to kid him into remaining at the line until his number is called—the command will come to be meaningless noise to the dog. Many handlers show that their dogs have come to this stage by the way they repeat "Stay" at the line so many times, each time louder than the last: "Stay . . . Now stay . . . . Listen to me, now—stay . . . Stay . . . Staaaaaay," and on and on.

As in singles and doubles, it is a good idea to let your dog's water work in triples lag behind his land work. A water triple of any length is a very tough test because the dog has to remember the falls such a long time, and it is nearly impossible to correct him for switching in water, so don't tempt him too strongly until he has been thoroughly switchproofed on land.

Here again, it should be stated that the above training tips do not constitute a complete program for teaching triples. The intent has been to discuss a few problems that are not adequately covered elsewhere, and to offer a few fresh approaches for dealing with those problems.

Handling Techniques

HUNTING SITUATIONS

What has been said about double marks applies to triples also. Most opportunities for triple retrieves will probably come while you are hunting ducks over decoys, and you must remember two important things: 1) have your dog located where he can see all the falls, and 2) be sure that he stays there until you send him to retrieve. You will also get an occasional triple while jump shooting, especially if the ducks were really relaxed when you surprised them. In those circumstances, a few stragglers will give you an additional shot. In jump shooting, your dog has to stay at heel if you are to do any shooting at all, and if he is to mark all the falls, he should stay with you until you send him to retrieve.

Multiple marks are also common in dove hunting around

Figure 38. The end of a good day's hunt. When hunters use two dogs in one duck blind, both dogs must be able to honor.

ponds, and the falls can be anywhere—on land, in water, or both—for the birds come from everywhere and fly away in all directions. A dog can get some real marking experience while dove hunting, but be sure that he stays wet, so that he doesn't become overheated. If most of your birds are falling on land, toss a dead bird into the pond now and then to give the retriever a chance to cool off.

Multiple marks can occur while walking up doves along hedgerows. Here you should keep the dog at heel until it is time to retrieve. If you let him range ahead of you, he won't flush any birds you won't flush yourself, and he is very likely to become overheated. Even if you keep him at heel, you should know where the nearest body of water is before you start out, so you will be able to take the dog to it if necessary. Frankly, it is probably better to do this kind of hunting without a dog than it is to risk a good retriever's life in the early season heat. As I mentioned earlier, I know a man who lost an excellent field trial dog this way. They were hunting doves a long way from water. The dog became overheated and died before they reached water. That dog had been placing in both the amateur and the open stakes at licensed trials.

I suppose some people encounter an occasional triple while hunting pheasants. I never have. There have been three birds in the air in front of me now and then, but I usually shoot a "two-tubed fowling piece," so I would have to hit two birds with one barrel to get a triple. On occasion I have toted a pump or autoloader and have had three birds to shoot at, but I more often came up empty than with a triple. Three pheasants provide a lot of excitement at one time. If I ever get a triple, you can bet that the dog will retrieve only the first one normally. The other two will be "Hunt 'em out" affairs. I would rather have an unsteady dog retrieve that first one for sure than have a steady dog lose all three of them for me.

FIELD TRIAL HANDLING

What has been said about letting the dog locate all guns on the way to the line applies more to triples, if that is possible, than it does to doubles and singles.

The proper way to set a dog up at the line for a triple is more complex. Generally, if both memory birds are on the same side of the field, you should set your dog up facing between them, possibly favoring the first to be thrown. If they are the two outside birds, you should have him almost facing the first one thrown, and

Figure 39.   A golden brings in a duck during a licensed field trial. The judges watch as the dog approaches the line.

then rotate your own body to indicate that he is to look around at the other memory bird as it is thrown. Your dog will come to interpret your movements correctly.

Like singles and doubles, the triple marked retrieve has no rule that says you have to send your dog as soon as your number is called. Give him a second, if necessary, to concentrate on the diversion fall. If he swings his head back to one of the memory birds right after the diversion hits the ground, encourage him to return his attention to the diversion before you send him. Never send him when he is looking in the wrong direction. See that the dog is looking at the diversion, and then give him a chance to concentrate before you say "Back!" Little things like this make a big difference in the way your dog performs in a field trial, and this kind of training will show in the number of times your dog places over the long haul.

As your dog returns to you with the first bird, you should turn to face the second bird he is to retrieve, but which one will that be? Two birds are still out there. Most of the time, you should have the dog pick up whichever bird he wants to next. It will be the one the dog is most certain of, the one he is thinking about. How do you know which one that is—especially while the dog is still approaching you with the first bird? If you watch him all the way back, you will see him glance at one of the other falls several times as he comes in. That is the bird he wants to retrieve, the one you should be facing when the dog reaches you. It's that simple: watch your dog all the way back, and he will tell you.

Some trainers will not do this with advanced dogs in very difficult triples. Instead, they select each bird for their dogs based on how they think the dog will score best. You will even see them select a memory bird as the first bird to be retrieved, even before the diversion. This is very advanced work, and the dogs are properly trained for it as well as thoroughly experienced in triples. Some tests can best be handled this way, if the dog is properly trained. When you need this kind of work, or think you do, go to a competent professional for advice about whether or not your dog is ready for it. If the answer is no, ask the pro to guide you in preparing your dog for this work. If the answer is yes, ask the professional to guide you through the training and handling necessary for it. Don't make this decision yourself, and don't attempt this training without professional assistance. You can completely confuse your dog with the wrong approach, especially if you start this kind of training too soon.

By the time you start working on triples, you will also be doing blind retrieves. Triples are sometimes run in the derby stake, of course, but most triple retrieve work occurs in the qualifying, amateur, and open stakes, where blind retrieves are required. In those stakes you will see people handling their dogs to marks, much as they do in blind retrieves. You will wonder if you should be doing this, and if so, when. Frankly, there is no simple answer to these questions. I can suggest a few guidelines, however.

In general, you should remember that a dog will always be penalized for being handled on a mark. Marking tests are run to test the dog's marking ability, and the person who handles a dog on such a test is saying to the judges, "My dog cannot find the bird without my assistance." The dog, in a sense, fails the marking test as soon as his handler blows the whistle the first time to stop him.

Considering that, the answers to two questions—"Should I handle on a mark?" and "When should I handle him, if at all?"— become a little clearer. Obviously, you should handle only when and if it will allow your dog to avoid a more severe penalty. If the dog will fail the test without being handled, and thereby be dropped from competition, then clearly he should be handled even though he will be penalized for it. For example, if the dog is about to switch—an action for which he will be dropped from competition—it is a good idea to handle him to the bird. With "clean handling" (one or two promptly accepted whistles), he may be called back for the next series; if he switches, he has no chance of continuing.

If you are certain that your dog will never find the bird without being handled, by all means take your penalty and blow the whistle.

These are about the only instances that can be clearly defined, however. Beyond these, you face a judgment call, and different handlers call things differently. You must consider several factors as you think about blowing the whistle.

Some judges view handling on a mark more seriously than others do. Whether we like to admit it or not, judging is not and never will be standardized as long as judges are mere human beings and not gods. Each judge is biased by his or her own experience, likes, and dislikes. A judge who has had dogs that were good markers but poor handling dogs may be tough on handling on a mark—or may be highly impressed by really good handling. Who knows? A judge who has been thrown out of a trial recently for handling on a mark may unconsciously seek revenge on the next handler who does the same thing, or the judge may do just the opposite and hardly penalize the handler at all.

Your own goals in this particular trial are another consideration. If you will be satisfied with a JAM (Judge's Award of Merit), you will be more inclined to handle than you will if you feel that anything but first place is a waste of your time. If, for example, you have a dog that needs only a first place to become a field trial champion or an amateur field trial champion or to qualify for one of the nationals, you will be less inclined just to stay alive by a handling. If nothing but first place means anything to you, why bother handling?

The work of the other dogs in competition is also a consideration. The judges are there to judge the relative merits of the dogs entered, not to judge all dogs against some mythical perfect retriever. If all the other dogs are being handled on this test, you will risk less by handling your dog than you would in a trial where no other dogs are being handled.

Timing is critical, too. Handling in the first series or in the last will probably hurt you more than handling in the middle series. In the first series, handling could get you dropped if not many other dogs are being handled. The first series is a weed-'em-out affair, whether we like to admit it or not. Errors there are heavily penalized. Similarly, errors in the last series are fresh in the judges' minds when they place the dogs. I remember a trial in which I ran both Duffy and Brandy. Duffy ran a sloppy trial in the middle series, but did very well in the first and last. Brandy ran an excellent trial, except that I had to handle him on the last bird of the last series. He handled well, getting the bird with just two whistles. Duffy received a JAM, which was more than he deserved. Brandy received absolutely nothing, although he ran a much better trial than Duffy did. Duffy, however, made his mistakes in the middle of the trial whereas Brandy made his on the very last bird, and the judges remembered his error too well.

Now that we have discussed the factors to consider, let's talk about what your dog will most likely be doing while you are making your decision as to whether or not to handle him. He will probably be out of the area of the fall, and you will be trying to decide whether he will be penalized more for wandering around out there or for being handled. Your decision will be more difficult if you feel that your dog will eventually come back into the area and find the bird without your assistance.

Dogs are penalized for being out of the area of the fall because they are disturbing too much cover. In hunting, such dogs could flush birds out of gun range—hence the penalty. The question is, when does this penalty exceed that for handling on a mark for these particular judges with these particular competitors, these particular personal goals, at this particular time in the trial?

This is a tough question, and no one else can answer it for you. As you gain experience, you will become more certain what to do, and you will probably do different things for different dogs (dogs are a variable, too). One dog will be totally lost when he goes out of the fall area, and you might as well handle him quickly and get it over with. Other dogs are scramblers and always seem to find their way back into the game, given a little latitude.

When you are doing triples (except in the derby stake), you will also be honoring other people's dogs. It is always a shame to see a dog that has been doing good work, possibly good enough to win a trial, blow it all by failing to honor in the last series. I remember one trial that Brandy won years ago. There was an honor on the last series, a water triple. Brandy is always a little hyper, and he squirmed quite a bit on the honor. I knew he wouldn't break, but the judges didn't, of course. After his honor was over, one judge told me that she had felt like standing on Brandy's tail, because she was afraid he would break—and he was a clear winner if he didn't. She needn't have worried, for Brandy was very steady on honor. In fact, I don't think he ever broke on honor in his life—in a trial, that is.

There is one other point about honoring that I haven't mentioned before: when the judge tells you that you may leave, always turn *toward* your dog as you heel him away from the line. If you turn away from him, he may break, but if you turn toward him, you will be blocking him with your body. I once saw a dog eliminate himself from a trial he was winning by breaking in this way. The handler turned away from him, and after a couple of steps the dog saw the working dog coming in with a big rooster pheasant in its mouth. The honoring dog not only broke but also started a donnybrook with the working dog over the pheasant. By turning *toward* this dog, the handler would have taken him the other way and also blocked his view of the working retriever. Unfortunately, however, the handler turned away from the dog.

Once again, as you leave the line, thank the judges.

Training Tests

The rest of this chapter is devoted to diagrams and explanations for triple marked retrieve training tests. The problems that arise from the placement of the three falls are the major concern here. Cover, terrain, and wind problems are covered in Chapter 1, "Single Marked Retrieves." Only where these environmental considerations create a special problem in a triple will they be discussed in this chapter.

Relatively simple triples are sometimes seen in derby stakes, but most often the triple is the marking test in the all-age stakes. Frequently there will also be one or more blind retrieves in the all-age stakes. Mixed marks and blinds are covered in Chapter 5, "Suction Blind Retrieves." As you review the triples in this chapter, however, you should remember that one or more blind retrieves can be set up with it in any all-age stake.

Triples seem to get longer and tighter every year. Tests that were considered difficult in the open stake a few years ago are now routine in the qualifying stake. I recently heard a qualifying stake handler quip that if the tests keep growing more difficult, judges should start awarding a Qualifying Field Trial Champion title similar to the Amateur Field Trial Champion title. Tests are becoming tougher because better dogs are being bred and better training techniques are being developed. Judges now have more difficulty finding a winner.

Occasionally a quadruple mark—with four birds—will occur in a field trial. These marks are not covered in this book because they are still relatively rare and because by the time your dog masters all the triples here, he will not have much trouble moving on to quads, if that is what you want him to do. Finding the fourth bird just puts a little more strain on the dog's memory—or on the handler's whistle if the dog cannot stretch his memory that far.

Figure 40 shows the eight different ways in which the birds can be thrown in a triple mark. In a single the birds can be thrown only two ways: left or right. The birds in a double can be thrown four ways: both outward, both inward, both left, and both right. In the triple, however, the birds can be thrown in eight different ways, and there are sixteen patterns for the quadruple. Each time you add a bird to the test, you double the number of possibilities. A mathematician would tell you that 2^n combinations exist where n represents the number of birds in the test.

Triples contain four sets of mirror images. The pattern in Figure A–1 is a mirror image of that in A–2; in A–1 all three birds are thrown to the handler's left, while in A–2 all are thrown to the handler's right. Figures B–1 and B–2 are mirror images of each other, too, as are C–1 and C–2, and D–1 and D–2. Dogs do not understand mirror images, however, so you must use all eight patterns in training your dog to do triples. You cannot let him come to expect any bird always to be on the same side of the gun; the dog has to mark the bird, not find it by rote.

In addition to the throwing patterns, you must consider

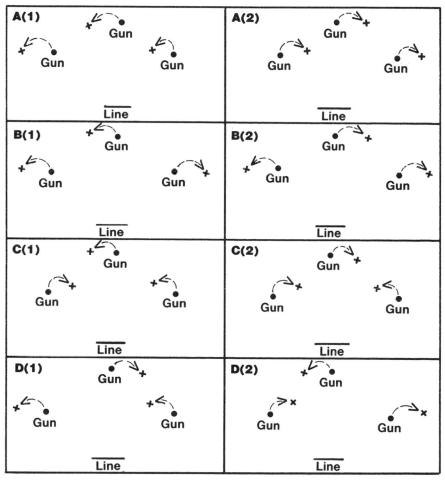

Figure 40. Throwing patterns for triple marks.

throwing sequences. The birds can be tossed in six sequences: left-middle-right, left-right-middle, middle-right-left, middle-left-right, right-left-middle, and right-middle-left. These sequences can have even greater significance than do the patterns, and your dog must be trained for each of them. The sequences also influence the way you set your dog up at the line before you call for the birds. You should normally have your dog sitting so that he faces a spot between the two memory birds (the first two thrown). This gives him a better look at the falls. If they are the outside birds, as in the left-right-middle and right-left-middle sequences, you should sit your dog facing halfway between the first memory bird and the middle bird, and then encourage him to shift around for the second throw. Do this by turning your own body that way between throws.

The guns in Figure 40 are all about the same distance from the line and about the same distance from one another. These distances also can be varied. The guns can be moved to different distances from the line and closer to or farther from one another—in an almost infinite number of combinations. Triples can be long or short or a combination of both; they can be tight or wide open. Consider all of these combinations before you worry about terrain, water, and cover. As you can see, there is no way to cover all of the possibilities for triples. Field trial judges come up with new ones fairly often.

You can, however, be sure that your dog is ready for all of the throwing patterns and throwing sequences. You can also expose him to a wide variety of length and angle variations in many different cover situations. After you have run in a few trials, or hunted for a few seasons, you will devise situations of your own to work on.

The distance between the marks and the line in triples depends on the same factors as those discussed in Chapter 2, "Double Marked Retrieves": your personal goals for your dog, your dog's experience level, visibility considerations, and the distance between the falls.

SHORT MIDDLE BIRD

Figure 41 illustrates a triple that offers many possibilities. The outside birds are long, and the middle bird is quite short. This test can be used effectively on both beginning dogs and experienced dogs in the same training session. All it takes is a change in the throwing sequence.

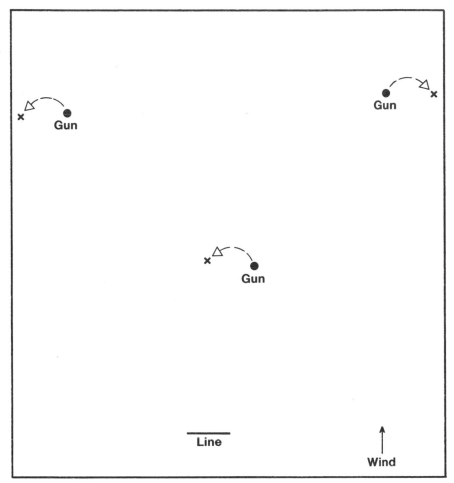

Figure 41. Short middle bird.

For the dog just starting to train for triples, this one should be thrown left-right-middle or right-left-middle. Either way, the short middle bird is thrown last; it is the diversion, and the dog will pick it up first. He should get it very quickly, so that he still remembers the other two marks very well. In any dog's early triple training you will do well to use short diversion birds for this reason.

For the more advanced dog, you should change the throwing sequence to middle-left-right or middle-right-left. This gives the dog a short memory bird. Such a bird will cause problems in double marks, as we have already mentioned. It also gives many dogs trouble in a triple. The dogs have to make *two* long runs after the outside birds before they attempt the short middle retrieve. Most dogs that are not used to this kind of test will just start running for the middle bird and will go out about as far as the outside falls before they start to hunt at all. The first time I ran into this test in a field trial, I couldn't believe the way my dog overran the short, seemingly easy middle bird. I was so astonished that I let him run almost to the next county before I blew the whistle and started handling him back to the bird. I must have waited too long, for we were not called back for the next series.

Some people train their dogs to pick up the short bird first, no matter what the throwing sequence is. This is a good idea for the dog that just cannot adjust to this test, but it should not be attempted until the dog is completely comfortable doing basic triples. If his memory is still not very good, don't confuse him with this kind of fancy exercise. Let him pick the birds up in any sequence he is comfortable with, and don't throw short memory birds for him until he is very confident.

For advanced dogs, this test can be set up in a crosswind. That way, scent from the short memory bird will blow to him as he goes after one of the long birds. If he turns and picks up the short bird, you may have difficulty getting him to go back out after the bird he first started after. Dogs tend to think that the bird they picked up under such circumstances is the one they originally started out for. Why this happens, I don't know, but it does. Once a dog veers off on his way to a particular bird and retrieves another, he will probably have to be handled to pick up the bird he originally started for. Thus it is a good idea to run an experienced dog on such a test occasionally. Avoid it with the green dog, however, for he has his hands full just trying to remember three falls.

It is not necessary that the short bird be the middle one, of course. All of the above applies if the short one is the left or right bird.

This test has all the character it needs without a lot of terrain and cover complications, but you can add any of those discussed in Chapter 1 if you want to.

Naturally, this test can be run in water as well as on land.

INVISIBLE NUMBER TWO BIRD

In Figure 42 we have a very widespread triple. In fact, there are about 90 degrees between the birds all the way around. This test is so wide that it shouldn't give even the greenest of dogs any trouble at all, provided he sees all three falls. That, of course, is the problem—getting your dog to see all three falls.

This is really more of a test for the handler than for the dog. Let me explain.

The inexperienced handler will bring the dog to the line and

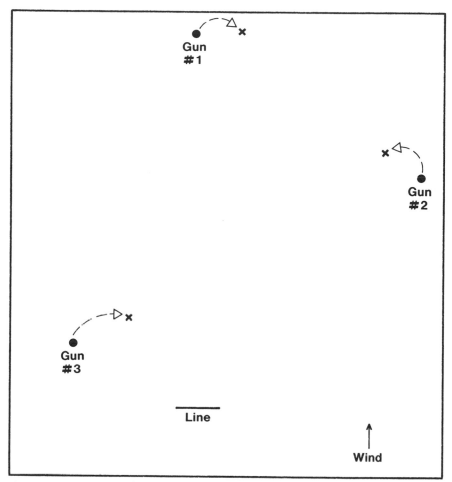

Figure 43. No two alike.

have him sit facing the middle (number one) bird. The dog will realize that a flier is in the making off to his left. He will know this when he sees three people and some bird crates over there. As we have mentioned, dogs get excited about fliers. Once he spots a flier, the average dog devotes most of his attention to it, giving the other birds only a casual glance as they are thrown. What the dog really wants to see is the bird that flaps its wings before it is shot. That is where the excitement is.

A flier will distract a dog from the other marks in any test. In this particular exercise, however, the flier can keep him from seeing the number two bird at all. If the dog is facing the middle bird, he will look at it as it is thrown and then swing his head back to face the flier, expecting it to be next. He knows that it is coming, so he will be reluctant to look away from it. While he is sitting there staring holes through the person who is about to throw the flier, the number two bird is thrown, 180 degrees away. Some dogs will not look around at the number two bird at all; others will look, but not in time to see the fall. In either case, the dog does not see the number two bird. Immediately after that, the flier goes up.

Such a dog will pick up the flier and then will undoubtedly go after the middle bird. Since he didn't see the number two bird, he will have to be handled to it. Being handled on a mark is a mistake in a field trial. Marking tests are supposed to test the dog's marking ability; there are blind retrieves to test his handling ability.

The more experienced handler will use a couple of techniques to ensure that the dog sees the number two bird. Incidentally, the handler must use both of these techniques *before* the first bird is thrown.

First, the handler will heel the dog to the line along a path that will allow the dog to see all three sets of guns before reaching the line. In fact, the handler will probably make sure that the flier is the last one the dog sees, just to be sure he sees the other two. Pro Jim Robinson was a staunch advocate of giving the dog a good look at all the guns before getting to the line. He drilled this into his clients in training sessions until it became second nature to all of us—even hardheaded me. I might mention that Jim has about as good a set of techniques for handling a dog at the line as anyone I have ever seen. If you ever have an opportunity to watch him, do so. If you imitate him, you will become a better handler.

If your dog finds all the guns before he reaches the line, you will never need to go through one of those embarrassing "Heel. Now mark it . . . No, heel . . . *Heel. Now mark it, goddammit!"* routines for every set of guns. Frankly, I believe that the use of such routines should be penalized as severely as barking and whining at the line and for the same reason: you cannot do that in a duck blind and get away with it.

The second technique the experienced handler will use is to position the dog so that he faces a spot *between* the number one and number two bird and does not face straight at the number one bird. This makes it easy for the dog to swing from the number one to the number two fall, rather than around to the flier. There is no way that the dog is going to miss seeing the flier, no matter how he is positioned. The flier is the bird he really wants anyway. The trick is to get him to look at the other two birds. Positioning him so that he faces between those other two will facilitate this.

Some handlers carry this technique a little further and try to keep their dogs from seeing the guns for the flier at all until after the other two birds are on the ground. For most dogs this is too much of a good thing. Of course, when the dog hears the shots for the flier, he will undoubtedly look around in plenty of time to mark the fall, but he might also break if he is not expecting a third bird. It is best to let most dogs know how many birds there will be in the test before they get to the line.

This type of test can be set up in water as well as on land, and sometimes the echo of the various shots from all three directions causes confusion. The dogs cannot seem to tell which direction each shot is coming from as a result of all the echoes.

NO TWO ALIKE

Figure 43 shows a triple in which each bird is thrown at a different distance from the line. This will test whether the dog is really marking the falls or just running by rote to some predetermined distance.

The dog will pick up the short number three bird rather easily. Then he will most likely go after the number two bird on the right-hand side. Many dogs will take the two outside ones before the middle if either was thrown last, as in this test. The number two bird is quite a bit farther from the line than is the short bird the dog picked up ahead of it. It is also thrown so that, in combination with the long middle bird, it offers a strong temptation to switch. These two are thrown toward each other. They can be widespread or snugged-up according to the dog's ability to handle switching problems.

The number one bird is quite far from the line. After the dog has picked up the other two—and particularly if he has had much of a hunt for either or both of them—he may have difficulty remembering where this first bird was thrown. Since it is also in a switching configuration with the number two bird, if the dog doesn't have it fairly well marked, he could stumble into trouble while hunting for it.

You can complicate this test for the more advanced dog by changing the throwing sequence to either left-right-middle or right-left-middle. These two sequences provide interesting short memory bird tests to the dog that is ready for them. If the middle bird is a flier, the dog will almost always get it first when it is thrown last, even if it is the longest bird. Even if the short left-hand bird is not a flier, some dogs will pick it up first no matter what the sequence may be.

Even when you use the basic middle-right-left sequence shown, you can toughen this test by using a flier as either the middle or the right-hand bird. No rule says that the flier *has* to be the last bird thrown. If either the middle or the right-hand bird is a

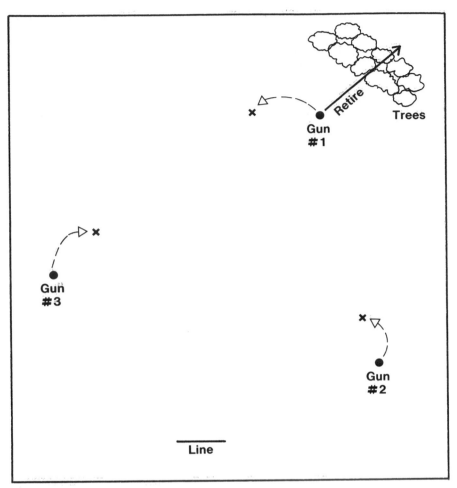

Figure 44. Hide 'n' seek.

flier and the throwing sequence is middle-right-left, the dog may not mark the short left-hand bird very well. He may even go after the flier first and thereby complicate his job considerably. He will leave himself with one long and one short mark, neither of which he took a very good look at. Many dogs have to be handled to both.

This type of test can be set up in water, too.

HIDE 'N' SEEK

A basic retiring-gun test appears in Figure 44. The gun for bird number one retires behind the trees after throwing the bird. Actually the gun waits until the dog has been distracted by the number two gun.

This type of test will show whether the dog is marking the

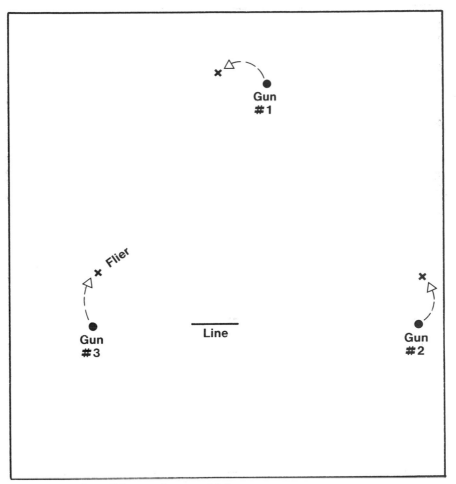

Figure 42. Invisible number two bird.

gun rather than the bird. If he is, he will have trouble finding bird number one; if not, he will have no trouble with it at all, especially in a simple test like the one shown here.

To train a dog for this test, you should have the gun retire only on reruns for quite a while. Set up the test and run your dog on it once or twice with the gun remaining in place. Run him this way until the test itself is old hat to him. Then run him again and have the gun retire after throwing the bird. If the groundwork was properly done, the dog should have no trouble. If he has problems, run him again with the gun staying in place.

Do not run the dog on a retiring-gun test until he has had many, many experiences with such patterns on reruns—different tests in different places over a period of time.

There is no reason to delay this work until your dog is doing triples. When he is doing good work on doubles, and when he is completely broken of any tendency to switch, retire the memory bird gun in the doubles *on reruns only* every chance you get. This will actually improve the dog's marking ability, for he will become less dependent on the presence of the gun.

This test can be set up in water as well as on land.

ONE BY SEA—TWO BY LAND

Figure 45 shows a triple retrieve in which the middle and right-hand birds are on land and the left-hand bird is in water. The throwing sequence is middle-right-left.

The dog must first swim after the water mark. Since dogs do

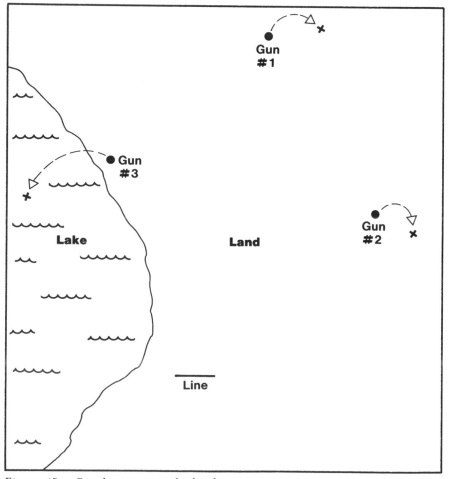

Figure 45.   One by sea—two by land.

not travel as rapidly in water as they do on land, it takes longer to complete this retrieve than it would a similar one on land. This taxes the dog's memory of the other two falls. The longer the swim, the tougher the test. Naturally, if this water mark is a flier or a shackled live duck, the test will be even tougher.

The other two marks can be as simple or as difficult as you wish to make them. Let your dog's ability guide you.

Incidentally, this is an excellent test for the dog that is about to start learning water triples. Water triples are more difficult than similar land triples because the dog has to remember each bird so much longer. You can ease your dog into them by running him on tests with only one bird in the water, and then on tests with two birds in the water, before you give him any triples in which all three falls are in water. This builds his confidence and keeps him out of trouble during the learning stages.

IN MEDIO STAT VIRTUS

In Figure 46 we have a water triple with considerable character, most of it centered on the very simple middle bird.

The dog will ordinarily go after this middle bird first since it is the last one thrown. This is an easy retrieve, straight across the water and up on the land. It presents no problem at all, but how it complicates the other two marks!

Most dogs will go after the right-hand (number two) bird next. It alone of the three fell into the water. The dog watches two of the three falls come down on land; then he retrieves one of them from the land. If he has not marked the number two bird very well, he will need a good deal of luck to find it without help. The dog that doesn't mark it well will normally plow right past it, reach land, and hunt all over for the bird until the handler blows the whistle and handles him back to it.

The dog that picks up both the number two and the number three bird will then face the long number one bird off to the left. To get to it, he has to take an angled path across the water and then hunt on land on the left side of the creek. If he gets lazy and goes straight across the water, as many partly trained dogs do, he will be right back in the area of the number three bird. With the creek blocking his way to the number one bird, he will most likely just mill around in the number three bird's area again.

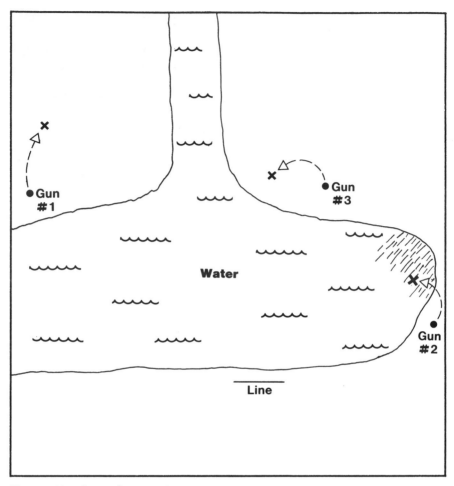

Figure 46.   In medio stat virtus.

That simple middle bird really complicates this test. *In medio stat virtus*—in the middle stands strength (the strength of this test).

4. BASIC BLIND
RETRIEVES

Training Tips

A basic blind retrieve is a test in which the dog does not see a bird fall but is handled to it with whistle and arm signals.

There are two whistle signals: (1) one sharp blast to get the dog to stop and look at the handler for directions; (2) one long and two short blasts (typically) to get the dog to come toward the handler. There are three arm signals: (1) the "Over," to direct the dog to the left or right (depending on which arm is used); (2) the straight "Back," to send the dog farther from the handler (either arm raised straight up); (3) and the angled "Back," which is halfway between an "Over" and a "Back."

A basic blind retrieve is run cold; that is, the test includes no other parts such as marks or other blinds. Many call these tests "cold blinds," meaning that they are run all by themselves. Cold blinds may be run in water, on land, or on a combination of both. Water blinds are typically more difficult than land blinds, just as water marks are more difficult than land marks. Water is a more difficult environment for the dog, no matter how much he enjoys it.

Blind retrieve tests, in which marks or other blinds are included, are covered in Chapter 5, "Suction Blind Retrieves." Whenever a test includes more than one blind or a combination of blind(s) and marks, part of the test is to determine whether the dogs will suck back to the fall or to the other blind. There are other forms of suction, of course, and they are all covered in Chapter 5.

This chapter is devoted entirely to cold blinds. It treats the problems brought into cold blinds by different wind, terrain, and cover conditions.

Blind retrieves are not allowed in the derby stake at field

Figure 47. A golden carrying a live duck. Most retrievers have very gentle mouths.

trials, but they are included in the all-age stakes. At this time, not one of the national breed clubs includes a blind retrieve in its working certificate program. That is unfortunate.

For the hunter, the dog's ability to do blind retrieves is second in importance only to his ability to do single marks. If I had my choice of a dog that could do doubles and triples to perfection or a dog that could do only single marks and cold blinds, I would hunt with the latter every time. Such a dog will bring back a far higher percentage of the birds I shoot than will the dog that does double and triple marks but not blinds.

Training for blind retrieves, especially at first, is best broken up into separate drills for each of the three parts: lining, stopping, and casting. Lining consists of sending your dog away from you initially when you start a blind retrieve. Stopping, of course, is necessary whenever the dog veers away from the line as he goes out; you stop him so that you can redirect him with arm signals. Casting is redirecting him with arm signals. You must teach each of these three skills separately before you can attempt real blind retrieves with any degree of success. This is a somewhat different training method from the one you use in marking tests, where the dog learns by doing.

Look at it this way: when you watch a good football team's practice sessions, you see something entirely different from what you see during a game. In practice, the players push sleds, run through tires, and drill on the many individual skills that add up to good execution. They seldom wear full pads; they scrimmage infrequently; they work on details most of the time. Then, during the game, they use all these details to produce a winning performance. So it is with retrievers being trained for blind retrieves. They are drilled on lining, stopping, and casting separately a good share of the time during training, and then all three skills come together when a blind retrieve is called for in hunting or in a field trial. To a great extent this is true all through a dog's life. He gets more drills than real blinds in training, not that he never gets any real blinds in training, for he does, just as a football team scrimmages occasionally. To stay sharp, however, the dog needs lots of drill.

Lining is taught with what we call "pattern blinds." A pattern blind is any blind retrieve in which the dog knows where the bird is before he is sent for it. This drill encourages him to run long straight lines. There are a number of different pattern blind techniques: the mowed-path variety, in which the dog is taught to run down paths mowed in the cover to get the bird, or the sight blind, in which the dog is heeled out to where the blind is, so that he can see it, and then heeled back to the line and sent for it. As a matter of fact, every rerun of a blind retrieve is a form of pattern blind, since the dog knows where the bird is and is being run just for drill on long straight lines.

My favorite is the cone pattern blind. In it, I use traffic cones to mark the location of the blinds so that the dog can see them from the line. To improve visibility, the cones should be white. Since they do not hold paint well, it is a good idea to cover them with white cloth sleeves. You can toss these sleeves into the washing machine now and then to keep them highly visible.

You must first teach your dog that the cone marks the location of the blind. To do this, put the cone out where you are going to plant the blind. Then bring your dog out and pick up several dummies. Heel your dog out to the cone and have him watch as you toss the dummies on the ground near the cone. Now heel your dog back 10 to 15 yards. Then turn around and send him toward the cone with your normal blind retrieve sequence—Dead bird . . . Line . . . Back, or whatever commands you use. The dog will run to the cone and pick up a dummy. As he is going away from you, run back farther from the cone, so that when the dog returns to you he will have a longer run to retrieve the next dummy. Keep sending him until he has picked up all the dummies, each one from a little farther away. Repeat this in different locations for several days, and your dog will come to associate the cone with the location of the dummies. Once he makes this connection, you will no longer have to heel him out to the cone and let him watch as you toss down the dummies. Simply put the dummies out when you position the cone. Your dog will know what the cone means when he sees it from the line.

After this initial conditioning, you can use the cones to set up any type of pattern blind you want to work on—uphill, downhill, across ditches, whatever—and be reasonably confident that your dog will retrieve correctly the first time. Each time you set up a new pattern, run your dog on it once or twice with the cone in place, and then remove the cone and rerun him two or three times without it. This conditions him to run blind without the cone. It also "pastes pictures in his album." Blind retrieves are memory tests to a greater degree than most of us realize. The dog stores up pictures of all the blinds he has ever run, and as he sits at the line he sorts through his album of pictures until he finds one that looks like what he is facing. If you can read your dog as you should, you will know when he does or does not have the right picture for a real blind. If he does, you send him. If he doesn't, you "No" him off the picture he has, reheel him, if necessary, let him find another picture, and so on.

Remember to run the dog once or twice with the cone in place, and then rerun him two or three times after you have removed the cone. If you never remove it, your dog will not come to know that blinds can occur without the cone. The cone simply helps him locate the position of the blind for the first run or two of each new pattern blind.

The cone also does one other thing: it teaches the dog to look out at the field when you set him up for a blind retrieve. So many dogs that are not trained this way will not look out. They just stare at the mud between their feet. Such dogs are difficult to handle, whereas the dog that is actively trying to form a picture is a joy to work with. A cone-trained dog will come to the line trying to get the picture. He will look out where you want him to, for the simple reason that you have given him something to see out there often enough in training. If he gets the wrong picture, you can "No" him away from it, and he will look for another one. He will eventually get the right one, whereas the dog that won't look out at the field will not get any picture at all. You will have to handle such a dog all the way out to the bird.

Pattern blinds should be rather long, at least 100 yards on land and 75 yards in water. You can use the cones in water patterns if you either stake them up in the water or put them on land behind the dummies, which should be in water as often as possible. Because pattern blinds are long, you run the danger of overworking the dog in any one training session. Be careful of this, for overwork can affect your dog's attitude toward this training if it happens often. Give him plenty of rest between runs. Actually, it is better to work with several dogs and rotate them.

Stopping is best taught when the dog is less than six months old. Teach him to turn toward you and sit when you blow a single blast on the whistle. If you drill him often when he is young, it will seldom occur to him later on that he can do anything but sit when he hears that whistle. Start with him on lead, of course, and keep him there for at least two months after you think he no longer needs it. If your dog is older, the technique is the same but not quite so easy to teach.

You can teach casting with the baseball technique described in James Lamb Free's book, *Training Your Retriever*. You can use the cones to improve this method considerably. Here again, once the dog understands that the cones mark the place where the dummies are located, you can set up all sorts of casting situations and have your dog handle them right the first time. Run him once or twice with the cones in place, and then rerun him two or three times after removing them, just as you did in the pattern blinds.

You should use these drills on lining, stopping, and casting all through your dog's life, not just until he is well enough trained to start running real blind retrieves. Your training program is just like the football team's practice sessions: you must drill, drill, drill on the details of proper execution so that they will all come together during the performance. If you skimp on any one part of the training, your failure to drill will show up sooner or later. I remember a Lab that ran field trials in my area many years ago. He was the finest marking dog I ever saw, and he had as much style and pizzazz as one dog could possess. He did very well in the derby stakes; in fact, he was *the* dog to beat wherever he went. He did not do too well in all-age competition, however, for the simple reason that he would not stop on the whistle consistently as he should have. In my opinion, this was the owner's fault. I frequently saw him running the dog on real blinds in training right after he was out of the derby, and the dog ignored whistle after whistle. The owner would just stand at the line and laugh about it instead of forcing the dog to obey. After about a year of this nonsense, the owner had unknowingly trained his dog to ignore the whistle entirely. Even after several months of professional training, the dog just could not be depended on to stop. He never did well in all-age competition as a result, and that was a shame, for he was one of the best animals I have ever seen. His one problem— ignoring the whistle—was totally man-made. Had his owner not been in such a hurry to move into real blinds, had he drilled this dog on the three elements of a blind retrieve, as described above, this problem would never have developed. With a different training approach, that dog might have become one of the all-time greats of his breed.

We so frequently waste time when we are in too much of a hurry. Sometimes we do irreparable harm to our dogs, too.

Let me make one final point about blind retrieve training: everything that has been said in the chapters on marked retrieves about letting water work lag behind land work applies even more significantly to blind retrieve training. Your dog should be thoroughly familiar with pattern blinds on land before you attempt them in water, and your dog should be reliable in casting drills on land before you try them in water. The reasons are the same as for marked retrieves: water is a much more difficult environment for the dog to work in, and you will not be able to get to your dog quickly to help him or to correct him.

The blind retrieve in water is such a difficult exercise and such an important one in retriever field trials that very few amateurs are able to train their dogs adequately for it without seeking professional help somewhere along the way. If your dog reaches a point at which he doesn't seem to be making any progress in his water blinds—and especially if his attitude toward working in water starts to deteriorate—by all means go to a competent professional for assistance.

One technique that I have used with great success in introducing a new dog to water blinds, and for keeping older dogs' spirits high through some of the more difficult phases of water blind training, is the thrown blind, which is described in the "Out-to-sea blind" test explanation (Figure 56). You can use this technique to introduce a number of different types of water blinds to your dog as he goes along, without allowing him to become discouraged with the work.

What has been said here is not a complete program for blind retrieves. The intent has been to present a few fresh concepts for handling some of the problems in teaching your dog to make blind retrieves.

Handling Techniques

HUNTING SITUATIONS

For dogs that can handle them, blind retrieves probably occur more often than any other type of retrieve, except the single mark. In an ordinary day's shoot, a dog has more chances for blind

Figure 48.   A proud moment. Young Bob Spencer with the first bird he ever shot—a dove. The golden, Duffy, had to make a blind retrieve in water to pick it up. Pat Spencer, who was too young to shoot, is in the background with the Labrador, Pepper.

retrieves than for double or triple marks, and frequently the blind retrieves are the birds that the hunter without a good dog would lose. Ducks that plop dead in the middle of the decoys can be picked up by anyone, but the one that sails 200 yards off and then collapses requires a dog, and a good one at that.

Duffy picked up the two most important birds in my hunting life with difficult retrieves, and one of them was a blind. These two birds, of course, were the first shot by each of my two sons. Bob, the older boy, hit a dove when the dog wasn't looking, and Duffy got it with a 40- to 50-yard water blind on a small pond, while both Bob and I looked on anxiously. If I had ever wondered whether the training for blind retrieves was worth it or not, I got the answer right then. Pat, the younger boy, shot a susie duck—hen mallard—that Duffy had to chase down as a lively cripple at a large impoundment, and he handled that job very well, too.

When you face a blind retrieve, it is very important that you be aware of the wind's direction. If there is a crosswind or a quartering wind, you should lead your dog into it enough to compensate for his inclination to drift with the wind as he goes out. You will seldom be hunting ducks directly into the wind; they don't decoy too well that way. Usually, you will have the wind at your back, which is ideal for blind retrieves, or blowing from one side or the other, which requires some allowance in the initial line you give your dog. If you fail to give him this lead, you will be faced with the need to have him take a cast directly into the wind at some point, after he has drifted some distance away from the true line to the bird. Getting a dog to take a good cast into the wind is very difficult, so you may lose the bird completely.

The next most important thing in handling your dog on a blind is to work him just as you do in training. Don't panic at the realization that this is a real situation, with a real bird at stake. Handle slowly and deliberately, just as you do in training. If you lose your composure and shout or gesture wildly, your dog will pick up your anxiety and will react poorly.

If you are hunting ducks over decoys, try to send your dog on a line that will keep him from becoming entangled with the decoy anchor lines. When setting out the blocks, leave a path for your dog to swim through. I forgot this once, and Duffy carried two of my favorite decoys out to sea, and I never saw them again. That is the smallest problem you could have if your dog becomes snarled in the decoy anchor lines. He could also drown or be intimidated by water for some time.

If the line to the bird is through the decoys, you have two choices. You can heel your dog down the shore to a point at which the line is not through the decoys, or you can give your dog a false line around the decoys and then handle him back to the correct line after he is past them. In a field trial, giving a dog a false line to avoid a hazard would be severely penalized, but in hunting you have only yourself to please.

Blind retrieves occur in the uplands, too, however. There you have an additional option: you can hurry your dog out to the area of the fall and command him to "Hunt 'em out." Frequently, this is the better choice, as far as probability of success is concerned. I use it frequently, even with the best-trained field trial dogs, simply because it brings back the meat more often than other methods do.

If there is a deep creek between you and the spot where the bird fell, however, you will have to make a genuine upland blind retrieve. The same is true if the bird falls on an island in a pond or lake. Here the same advice applies: know where the wind is, allow for it in the initial line you give your dog, and handle just as you do in training; don't become shrill in your anxiety to get the bird.

Try to remember one other thing in hunting blind retrieves:

start from a position that will allow you to see your dog all the way to the bird. You cannot know when to handle him if you cannot see him. Similarly, he cannot obey your arm signals if he cannot see you. If necessary, heel him to a rise in the ground before you send him. I have seen field trial judges forget this a few times and set up what I call "tall man" tests—those in which the handler has to be well over six feet tall to be able to see the dog some of the time. Being short myself, I strongly object to this kind of test, as I have mentioned to a few judges.

FIELD TRIAL HANDLING

In trials as in hunting, it is very important to know how the wind is blowing and to allow for it in giving your dog an initial line. You will see handlers tossing tufts of grass into the air as they wait their turns to run a blind retrieve test. This is more than just nervousness, although there is probably some of that in it, too; they want to know exactly how the wind is blowing.

Another important thing is knowing exactly where the blind is planted for your dog. As you stand in the holding blind just before you take your dog to the line, watch as the blind is planted. Naturally, your dog must not be able to see the location of the blind; that is against the rules. If you watch, you will avoid two problems: finding that the trial officials forgot to plant a bird for your dog, and failing the test because you didn't know where the bird was.

There is no penalty for running your dog when no bird is planted. You will be allowed to rerun with a bird there, and your dog will be judged only from a point near the bird on the rerun; his original work will be used to that point. This is as fair as they can make it, but the time you spent handling your dog to a nonexistent bird will be more than wasted. You will have had to handle too much. This could affect your dog's responses to handling in the next test, and it could influence the judges unfavorably no matter how they try to ignore it. None of this will happen if you watch the trial officials plant the bird for your dog.

If you aren't sure where the bird is planted, how can you handle your dog to it? I once saw a man fail in a field trial because he thought the blind was about 50 yards farther out than it was. He literally combed the area with his dog, which took every cast beautifully. The owner must have handled the dog for twenty-five or thirty times before the judges told him to pick the dog up, that he had failed the test. It is your responsibility to know where the

Figure 49. A blind retrieve in a field trial. The handler is giving his dog a "back" cast as one of the judges watches. Notice that the dog is turning to go back.

bird is, and you will be dropped if you fail to locate it with your dog as a result of your own ignorance of its position.

Assuming that you know *that* a bird was planted for your dog and exactly *where* it was planted, all you have to do is handle your dog to it as cleanly—that is, with as few whistles—as possible. Ideally you should "line" the blind, have your dog retrieve the bird from the initial line you gave him without further handling. If the wind is blowing from straight behind you, you should line the dog right at the bird, but if there is any kind of a crosswind or quartering wind, you will have to lead him an appropriate amount if you are to have a chance of lining the blind. If you lead him too much, you can be accused of "avoiding the test," but if you do it just enough so that the dog comes up very close to the bird before you have to handle him, or if he lines it himself, no one can say you avoided the test. You did it perfectly.

If some form of hazard is present, such as a point of land in a water blind, you will have to use your own judgment as to whether or not you should line your dog away from it. You will be penalized for doing so, and penalized more heavily the more you do it, for you are actually avoiding the test in giving your dog a false line away from the hazard. You have to decide what the probability is that your dog will fail the test if you don't give him the false line and how much his chances improve with a bit of a false line, and so forth. In making this decision, ask yourself once more all the questions that we discussed before. How do these particular judges feel about the false line? How are the other dogs doing? What are my personal goals in this trial? Which series is this? And so on. Handling a dog involves more than tooting a whistle and waving your arms. It takes experience and judgment, and a little bit of luck now and then.

When you reach the line, take all the time your dog needs to settle down and prepare for the test. You should line him up so that his spine is aimed along the line you intend to send him. He will run along the line of his spine, not necessarily in the direction in which his head is aimed, if the two directions are different. Once he is sitting the way you want him, give him time to form the right picture of the blind he is about to run. Blind retrieves are memory tests to a greater degree than we think. As we have said before, the dog stores up mental pictures of all the blinds he has been trained on or run on in trials, and he sorts through his "album" as he sits at the line. When he finds a mental picture that is similar to what he sees before him, he has a picture. It may be the right picture or the wrong one, but at least he has a picture. If it is the wrong one, you have to realize it and work him out of it, heel him again, if necessary, and let him find another picture until he finds one that you can see is approximately correct. Don't rush this process. You will earn no extra points for sending your dog as soon as you reach the line.

When you reach the line for a blind retrieve, you will find it useful to have a word that tells your dog that this is a blind, not a mark. I use "Dead bird." When I say those words, my dogs know that this is a blind retrieve. Other handlers say "Blind." When I'm certain that my dog has the right picture, or approximately so, I say "Line" as I put my hand down beside the dog's head to indicate that I agree with his picture and that I am about to send him. If I don't like his picture, I say "No" and do not put my hand down beside his head. Dogs pick up this routine very easily.

Once your dog has formed the correct picture, you must send him immediately. If you delay, he may decide that he has the wrong picture, and you may then have difficulty reestablishing it. I remember once when I was running Brandy in a licensed trial.

The test was a double land blind, and I had a difficult time getting
him to find the right picture for the first (shorter) bird. I had
heeled him around several times before he found the right picture. Just as he did, someone drove a big truck right into the middle of the test. One of the judges stepped up behind me and told
me that, if I wanted to, I could take my dog off the line until they
moved the truck. I looked down at Brandy and saw that he was
still locked in correctly. Then I looked up and saw that the truck
was not in a direct line to either blind. I knew that if I heeled
Brandy off the line, he would figure that he had the wrong picture,
and it would be difficult to set him up properly again. I had to decide quickly; there was no time to run all this data through a
mental computer. I gulped and said "Back!" The judge, who had
expected me to leave the line, gasped audibly. But Brandy lined
the blind and then found the other bird on one whistle, all to my
great delight. Afterward, the judge told me that I took a dangerous
chance but that maybe I did the right thing. Actually, all I did was
play the percentages. Even if the test had gone wrong, I would
have felt that I made the right decision.

Once you have sent your dog, the next big problem is knowing when to blow the whistle to stop him. As a general rule, don't
stop him as long as he is proceeding purposefully along the approximate line you gave him. If he veers off, starts to hunt, or pot-
ters around, however, blow the whistle and give him an appropriate cast.

Sometimes the appropriate cast is not obvious to the beginner. Frequently a new handler will try to give the dog an angled
"Back" when an "Over" is really called for. A series of poorly exe-
cuted angled back casts will score lower than a single over cast
followed by a single back, for example. It is important to change
hands when going from an "Over" to a "Back." If you follow a
left-hand "Over" with a left-hand "Back," your dog is likely to
continue the over cast instead of going back. Normally, a left-hand
"Over" should be followed by a right-hand "Back," and vice versa.
That is just the way dogs work.

A dog that takes an "Over" for only a short distance and then
turns and runs away from the handler, as in a straight or angled
"Back," is said to *scallop* or *scallop back*. This can be a real problem.

If your dog tends to scallop back on his "Over" casts, you can
get a decent "Over" from him in a trial by giving the "Over" arm
signal together with the "Come in" whistle. This is strictly an
emergency measure that depends on an element of surprise. If the
dog grows accustomed to it, it will do no good at all, so don't use it

in training; correct the beast for scalloping there (that's what training is for).

You should also know about hard "Over" casts. If you give an "Over" and use a loud voice and a vigorous arm movement, or perhaps even run a step or two in the direction of the "Over," your dog will most likely take an angled "Back." Sometimes this will work much better than the angled "Back" cast itself.

For most "Over" casts, however, a soft voice (or none at all) plus a slow arm movement and a couple of leisurely steps will work much better. One of the reasons that dogs tend to go to pieces in competition is that their inexperienced handlers change from the soft "Over" casts of training to the hard "Overs" of panic. If you really want to help your dog, handle him in trials exactly as you do in training—same tempo, same voice, same body movements.

One last reminder: don't go to the line without your whistles and your white jacket. Don't laugh—this happens frequently.

Training Tests

The rest of this chapter is devoted to diagrams and explanations of training tests for basic blind retrieves. These tests show how cover, terrain, and wind can be used to create problems in blind retrieves. Problems created by artificial hazards—marks, dry guns, decoys, and so forth—are covered in Chapter 5, "Suction Blind Retrieves."

Blind retrieves are not used in the derby, but they are required in each of the all-age stakes. They are the most crucial tests, in fact.

The blind retrieve had an unusual origin. In English field trials, a dog is sometimes asked to retrieve a bird that another dog has failed to find. Success in this kind of retrieve has always carried great prestige and is called "wiping the other dog's eye." Back in the early days of English field trials, a trainer named Dave Elliot searched for a reliable way to "wipe the eye." One day he attended a demonstration of how stock dogs were used to herd cattle and sheep. He noted that the handler used a whistle and arm signals to direct the stock dogs, and it occurred to him that the same technique might work with his retrievers. He tried it, and it did work—amazingly well. His technique caught on in England, and later, when he came to this country, he brought his handling dogs with him.

Whistles and arm signals, in other words, began as ways to help the dog pick up a mark that he couldn't find. They have come a long way from their original purpose. In fact, if they are used to help a dog on a mark now, a penalty will result. Dogs are expected to find marks without assistance. Handling is for blind retrieves, where the dog doesn't see the bird fall.

Many people regard blind retrieves and the handling that goes with them as the most interesting part of retriever field trials today.

ROAD HAZARD BLIND

Figure 50 illustrates a simple land blind containing one significant complication for the dog that has done pattern blinds on mowed paths. That complication is the road that runs diagonally across his path as he goes toward the blind. A road in this type of test is nothing more than a set of well-used tire tracks through the field; even a cow path will do. It should never be any kind of public road, street, or highway. Such thoroughfares are far too dangerous.

If the test is set up properly, the dog will have to run on the road for some distance as he goes toward the blind. If he then enters the cover again when the road turns, he has done well indeed. If he continues on the road—as do many dogs that have spent a lot of time on mowed-path pattern fields—the handler has a problem—a couple of problems, in fact.

The handler's first problem, of course, is handling the dog off the road and back onto the line to the blind. A straight or angled "Back" cast will probably not succeed. The dog is likely to turn and head farther down the road, for once he decides that he is on another mowed path, he will tend to stay on it. The safest cast to use here is a left-hand "Over." That will get him off the road, even if it sends him in the wrong direction. Once he is safely back in the cover, the handler can stop him and send him toward the blind with a right-hand "Back." It is usually advisable to change hands when giving a "Back" after an "Over." If the handler uses the same hand for the "Back" as for the "Over," most dogs will attempt to continue the "Over" cast instead of changing directions.

The second problem facing the handler whose dog stayed on the road too long is the fact that the dog probably lost his picture. Many dogs require a good deal of handling—hacking really— when they no longer have a picture of the blind they are running. This is especially true of dogs with a lot of "hunt" in them. Dogs

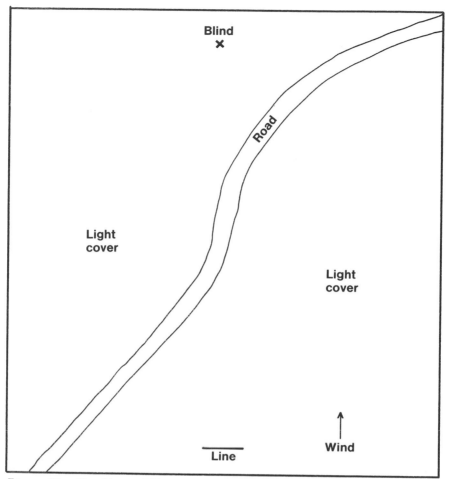

Figure 50. Road hazard blind.

without all this "hunt" will take long, straight casts and get out of this situation with fewer problems.

One thing this test demonstrates is the folly of training on mowed paths for pattern blinds. Dogs so trained will run on every road and path they come across in a blind retrieve, for that is what they have been trained to do.

UPHILL BLIND

The land blind shown in Figure 51 contains two complications, one for the dog and the other for the handler.

First, let's look at the dog's complication. The test is run straight up a fairly steep hill. It is best if the hill grows steeper as it goes up. The line is on flat ground some distance from the base of

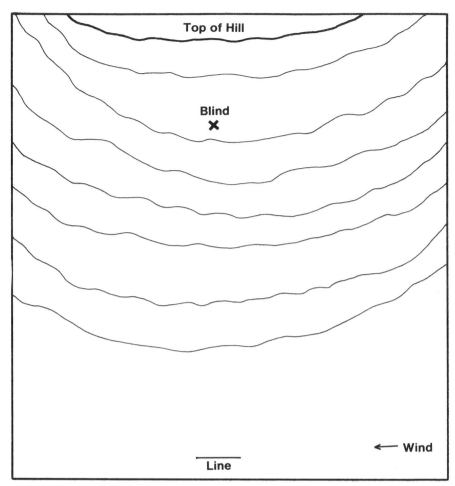

Figure 51. Uphill blind.

the hill. The dog will start at his normal pace, whatever that is. When he gets to the hill, he will slow down some as he starts to climb. The farther uphill he goes, the more he will slow down. If he has any pop in him at all, he will probably stop altogether and look around at his handler for an arm signal. (To "pop" means to stop and look for directions without a whistle signal from the handler.) Straight uphill blinds will bring out any tendency the dog has to pop. The terrain slows him down. If he is at all uncertain, he will finally give in, turn around, and sit down.

Popping can become a very serious fault. The dog can develop a habit of running a few feet and then popping, running a few more feet and popping again. Most young dogs will pop a few times before they become confident about blind retrieves. A dog that is rushed too much in blind retrieve training can develop a serious popping problem. If you have such a problem with your dog, don't hesitate to go to a pro for help in solving the problem before it becomes entrenched.

To prepare for this test, run your dog often on uphill pattern blinds in training.

Now, let's look at the complication this test has for the handler. It is run with a right-to-left crosswind. Most dogs will tend to "suck" with the wind; that means that they will not run a true line to the blind, but will drift off the line with the wind to some degree or another. Some dogs are worse about this than others, but they all do it. In such a test, if the handler lines the dog directly at the blind, the dog will drift off-line to the left as he goes out. This is further complicated by the fact that all dogs are very difficult to cast directly into the wind. This means that if the dog gets very far off-line, handling him back to the correct line will be difficult. I have seen handlers stop their dogs only 15 yards off-line and handle them several times with "Over" casts, only to have the dogs wind up 50 yards off-line. At each "Over," they moved a few feet in the proper direction and then turned and drifted with the wind again until the handlers blew the whistle once more. The time lag between a dog's error and the whistle and the second lag between the whistle and the response let the dog get farther off-line each time he was handled.

The solution to both of these problems—sucking with the wind, and not taking casts into the wind—is to lead the dog into the wind on the initial cast. Instead of lining him right at the blind, line him (in this instance) to the right of the blind. How far to the right? Far enough so that he will arrive very close to the blind without further handling, after being drawn slightly to the left by the wind. How far to the right you should line him up depends on the dog, and it is the handler's responsibility to know the dog well enough to give the correct line. If you think this is a problem for the one- or two-dog owner-handler, think about the professional with a string of perhaps twenty dogs, no two exactly alike in this or any other respect.

This uphill/crosswind blind is a good test because it tests not only the dog's performance but also the handler's knowledge of the dog.

ACROSS THE GRAIN

The land blind in Figure 52 is set up so that the dog has to take a diagonal line through a field of cut grain. Because each pair of rows of grain marks out a path, the dog will show a strong

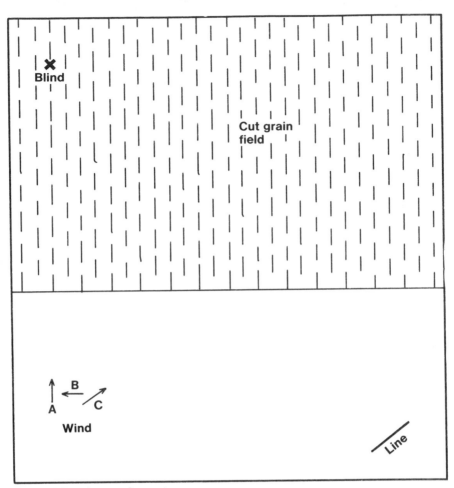

Figure 52. Across the grain.

tendency to run down the row rather than to continue on the correct line to the blind. Dogs trained on mowed paths are more susceptible than those not so trained, but all dogs will tend to do this. Wind direction can be a big factor in determining how to handle a dog in this test, so we will discuss it in relation to the different winds.

First, let's consider a windless situation, which rarely happens but does at least show this test in its most elementary form. With no wind, the only problem the handler faces is that of determining how far to the left (in this instance) to lead the dog in order to counteract the tendency to drift down the rows of grain. The distance will vary from dog to dog, and the handler must know his or her dog well enough to make the correct decision. In the windless situation, a little error one way or the other is not too serious, for the dog can be easily handled back onto the proper line.

With wind 52–A the correct lead becomes much more important, for this wind will not only intensify the dog's tendency to run down the rows but will also make it difficult to handle him back onto the true line once he strays. Trying to handle him over to the left will not involve direct into-the-wind casts but will be close enough so that his responses will be poor. It is better to lead him plenty, so that he winds up very near the bird on his initial cast. If he goes a little to the left of it, handling him from there will be no problem. If he goes very far to the right, he may never complete the test.

Wind 52–B is a friendly wind. It counteracts the dog's tendency to drift down the rows. Depending on how strong it is, this wind may force the handler to line the dog right at the bird or even to the left of it. Here again, the handler must know the dog.

Wind 52–C is a killer. It not only intensifies the dog's tendency to drift but also makes it very difficult to cast him toward the bird once he gets off line to the right.

The only way handlers can become familiar with their own dogs' lead requirements under these varying conditions is to train the dogs in similar situations often. Pattern blinds like this one are easy to set up. Very windy days—those days that are too windy for other kinds of work—are ideal for pattern-blind training. Not only can the trainers get a better idea of how their charges react but they can also in some instances train their dogs to drift a little less with the wind by running the dogs on pattern blinds in strong winds. Training for the various casts ("Back," "Over," "Come in") on blustery days is also a good idea.

TAKE COVER

The land blind illustrated in Figure 53 will show whether your dog will take the line you give him or wander off as he pleases. Between the line and the bird lies a patch of heavy cover. If your dog is well-trained to take the line you give him, he will plow right through that cover; if not, he will veer off to the right and avoid it.

What difference does it make, as long as he gets the bird? Well, it's mostly a question of control. In many situations it is important for your dog to take the exact line you give him—sometimes for his own safety, other times to avoid disturbing cover that may conceal game, and still other times because it is the only way he can actually get the bird. Although not every situation calls for this level of control, many do. Your dog will have no way of know-

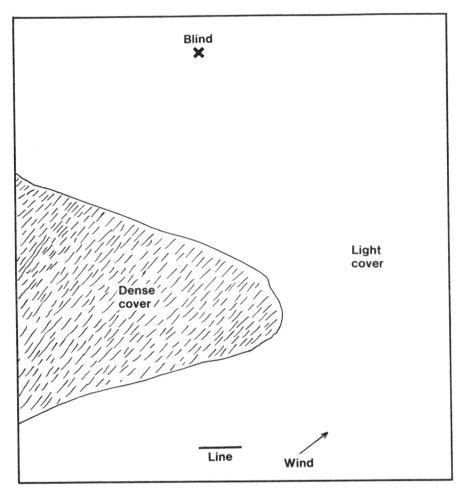

Figure 53. Take cover.

ing when he is to take your line and when he can improvise, so you should train him to take your line every time. This test will show whether or not you have done so.

To train for this test, you should start out right in the middle of the patch of dense cover. Run the dog to the mark two or three times from the cover. Then move back just out of the dense stuff but close enough so that he almost cannot avoid running through it, and run him a few more times. Gradually move farther and farther back, as the dog's success allows. In the early stages, building confidence is more important than setting up situations in which you can correct him for making a mistake.

Eventually he will make a mistake and go around instead of through the cover, and you must then correct him firmly. *Where* you correct him is very, very important. You should let him run about 60 yards in the wrong direction before you correct him. He will then be 60 yards from the line and off to the right of the blind a considerable distance—exactly where you do not want him to be and not near any place he should be in this test. Correct him there, and he will associate the correction with that place. That will make him try to avoid that place in the future, which is exactly what you want. To avoid that place, he will almost have to plow through the cover.

How do you correct a dog that is 60 yards away from you? Several methods are very effective, but so harsh that you should not learn them from a book. Ask a professional to teach you how to do this. The fee he charges will be money well spent.

This whole correction procedure is based on the dog's place consciousness as it relates to punishment. As I mentioned earlier, dogs, for reasons we don't fully understand, associate punishment with the place in which it occurs. You can let this help or hurt your training program, depending on where you punish your dog. Do it where he should not be, in the place you want him to avoid, and he will train easily. Do it in a place where he should go, and he will regress.

For this reason, do not ever, ever punish a dog near the line, no matter how serious an error he makes (unless he refuses to leave when you say "Back," and then you have to make the line an unpleasant place to be). If he goes at all, no matter how bad his line may be, do not correct him until he is at least 60 yards from the line. If you correct him before he has gone very far, he will be too near the line you gave him to understand what he is being corrected for. He will assume that he is being corrected for going at all. This can lead him to believe that he will be punished for going at all—a serious problem.

In this test the wind will encourage the dog to avoid the cover and will also cause him to drift off line after he gets through the cover as he goes toward the bird. For this reason, you will need to lead him to the left a little in giving him the initial line.

CROSS-CANYON BLIND

This downhill-uphill blind requires that the handler understand another canine peculiarity: the tendency to run straight downhill and straight uphill rather than angling down and up. Every dog will "square" the hill at some point going either up or down.

In this test, if you line the dog directly at the bird, he will

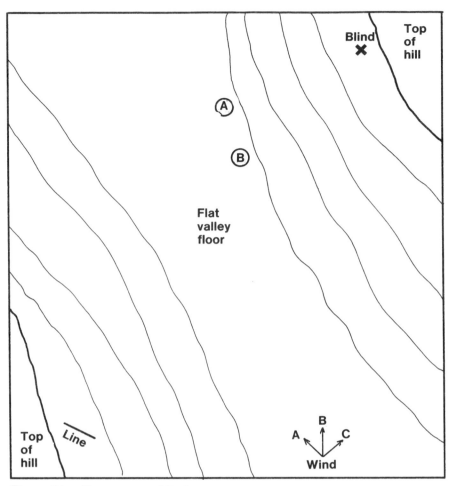

Inside figure labels:
Blind
Top of hill
(A)
(B)
Flat valley floor
Top of hill
Line
A B C
Wind

Figure 54. Cross-canyon blind.

have to angle down the near hill and then angle up the far hill in order to "line" the blind. If the hills are very long and/or very steep, no dog will do that. Once again, the dog must be given a false line somewhat to the left of the true line to the bird if he is to do well. In a blind retrieve, the wind is not the only factor that requires the dog to be led one way or the other; terrain can also necessitate this.

First, let's consider this test in a windless situation. You should give the dog an initial line that will allow him to reach the base of the far hill at point A. The reason for this is that he is going to run straight up the far hill no matter what the handler does, so it is a good idea to have him arrive at a point where that will be correct. Point A is such a place. A dog will follow an angled line up or down a hill for a short distance from the line, but he will not do it when he starts up that far hill. Instead, he will run straight up.

To direct him to point A, you must give him an initial line somewhat to the left of point A. Lining him somewhat to the left of the blind is not good enough. You must line him to the left of point A, too. Many handlers forget about the far hill and angle their dogs at point A. The dogs arrive at point B and "square" the hill (run straight up it) there, forcing the handlers to hack them to the bird with a series of "Over" and "Back" casts. This is sloppy work, and it is the handlers' fault for not giving the dogs the proper line in the first place.

Wind 54–A will help to counter the dog's inclination to square the hills. His tendency to drift with the wind will partially offset this inclination if the wind is mild to moderate. A really strong wind could completely nullify the tendency to square the hills, or overcome it and then some. Again, the handler is responsible for knowing how to work the dog, an understanding one gets from day-in-day-out training with one's dog.

Wind 54–B will diminish the dog's tendency to square the hills and will require a less lead than one has to use in a windless situation, unless the wind is a gale.

Wind 54–C will intensify the dog's tendency to square the hills. More lead will be required than for the windless situation.

Many different tests—sidehill-uphill blinds, sidehill-downhill blinds, long flat blinds with the bird planted halfway up a far hill, blinds with the line halfway down a hill and the bird a long way out on flat ground, and so forth—take advantage of this canine quirk. If you know your dog well enough to get through this cross-canyon test, however, you will be able to figure out how to handle the others, for they are all simpler.

Your dog's greatest asset is his nose, and you expect him to use it. Your greatest asset is your mind, and your dog has a right to expect you to use it as much as he uses his nose.

CROSS-CHANNEL BLIND

The problem with the blind shown in Figure 55 is that it is not straight across the channel. It is at an angle from the line. In a test like this most dogs will suspect that they are going to swim all the way across the channel and then land before finding the bird, unless their trainers have taken great pains to make them think otherwise—more about this later. If a dog thinks that the bird is on land, he will tend to swim straight across the channel rather than continue on the angled line the handler gave him.

There can be many reasons why the handler doesn't want the

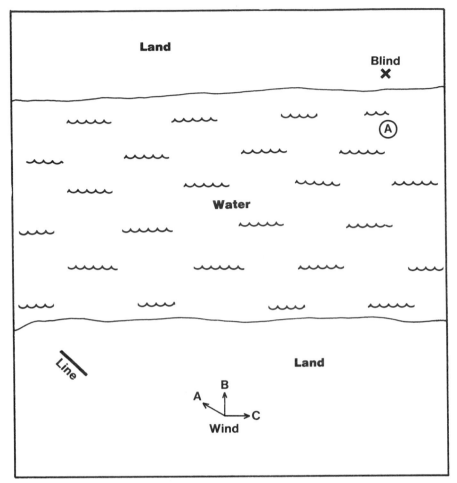

Figure 55. Cross-channel blind.

dog to go straight across the water. In a field trial, for example, swimming straight across is heavily penalized. In hunting, there may be a duck blind, with a dog—or any number of other things—over there. The basic reason for wanting the dog to take the line given him, however, is control. The handler either does or does not have control over his dog. There is no such thing as partial control, 80–20 control, or anything else like that. If the dog is under the control of his handler, he will continue on the line given him. If he isn't, heaven only knows what he might do at any given time.

To complete this test properly—under control—the dog must swim on an angled line across the channel. Most dogs will tend to turn into shore after swimming a certain distance if they expect the bird to be on land. For this reason, the trainer should almost never put the bird on land during training. It should be at point A, out in the water. If the dog expects to find the bird in the water, he will not be so eager to go ashore. That will help in training a dog to take good angled lines in water. Judicious correction as soon as he lands after he errs in training on this kind of test will also help, if it is not overdone to the point where the dog is afraid to go ashore. This kind of punishment is tricky, so the beginner should learn about it from a pro rather than from a book. Two points are worth making. First, the dog should never, never be corrected in the water, no matter how far off-line he is; correction should take place as soon as he lands. He will associate the correction with the place he landed—on shore, not with the water. Punishing a dog in water will only convince him that he should stay out of it, and that will cause serious problems.

Second, in a trial or in an actual hunting situation, it is best to give yourself a little insurance and lead your dog a little to the right of the true line to the bird. That way, if he bends in to the far shore a little, his performance won't suffer at all; if he doesn't bend, you can handle him very easily to the bird as he swims by.

The wind will affect the amount of lead you have to give your dog. Winds A and B will intensify your dog's tendency to hook into the far shore, so they will require more lead. Wind C will counteract that tendency, so less lead will be needed. Here again, it is up to the handler to know how much lead to give in each situation.

OUT-TO-SEA BLIND

Figure 56 illustrates a water blind that looks simple, but many dogs refuse even to try it. It is set up in a cove of a large impoundment lake. The bird is planted out in the main lake and the line is on the shore of the cove. From the line the dog can see nothing but water for two or three miles. Since most blinds are planted near shore, the dog is now forced to conclude that he is being asked to swim clear over to the other side of the lake for just one lousy duck. No wonder so many of them just lie down and curl up when their handlers say "Back." They seem to say, "Gee, boss, can't we drive around there for this one, or forget it altogether?"

The problem lies in the way we train our dogs—mostly on small bodies of water, with blinds either on the far shore or very close to it. Setting up tests like this one is difficult, so most of us never get around to it. Then when our dogs fail such a test during a trial or in hunting, we are bewildered—as bewildered as our dogs.

This is a real hunting test. Several years ago, when Duffy was

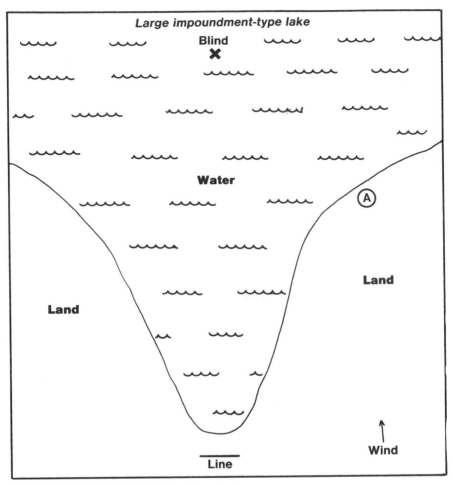

Figure 56. Out-to-sea blind.

a youngster, I took him hunting with a couple of non-dog-owning friends in a cove of a large impoundment. Shooting was good, and Duffy did two or three nice cross-cove blind retrieves, which impressed my friends considerably. With a minimum of encouragement, I found myself bragging about Duffy's abilities a little more than it is advisable to do before the end of the day. Then someone shot a duck that landed out in the main part of the lake, and Duffy didn't see it fall.

"No problem," I told them. "Just another blind retrieve for Duffy." I sat him down facing the right direction and said, "Dead bird . . . Line . . . Back!" Duffy just sat there. I went through the routine again. He hunkered down a little and didn't move. I became embarrassed, and did all the things a person does when he is showboating. We never did get that bird, and I didn't say much more about how great Duffy was the rest of the day. The worst part is that it took me a long time to figure out what the problem was. Duffy thought I was asking him to swim several miles, not 60 or 70 yards.

The best way to train for this type of test is with the thrown blind. Have an assistant hidden at point A in the diagram. He or she should have several big white dummies. Heel your dog to the line, and go through your blind retrieve with him. As you say "Back," signal to your assistant to throw a dummy to the spot where the blind is in the diagram. The dog will see it and swim out and retrieve it with no difficulty. It's just another marked retrieve at this stage. Next, delay the signal to your helper until the dog has gone to the edge of the water, where he is most likely to balk this time. Again he will see the dummy and swim out to retrieve it. Next time, delay the signal a little longer, until the dog has swum a few yards. Gradually lengthen the delay between sending him and signaling for the dummy until he is swimming all the way out. The next day, go to a different spot and start all over again. And so on.

There are several things to keep in mind when doing thrown blinds. First, be sure that your assistant is hidden from the dog at all times. The dog shouldn't see or hear your assistant from the line, while he is swimming out, while the dummy is being thrown, or while he is swimming back. I made the mistake of not keeping my blind throwers hidden when I trained Duffy, and that created a suction problem that it took a good pro some time and effort to cure.

Second, do not overwork the dog. These long swims take so much out of a dog that you should let him rest after about every other one. It is best if there are several dogs going through this training together so that one can work while the others rest.

Third, do not rush your dog. Do the work gradually so that he isn't tempted to refuse to retrieve and come back to you without the dummy. If you wait too long to signal your assistant to throw the dummy, your dog may become confused and turn around and return to you. As long as he is facing you, he cannot see the dummy when it is thrown, so you will have to handle him back to his original direction, which may not work at this stage because of his fright. If he gets all the way back to you without the dummy, you will have to go back several lessons, or maybe even start all over. It is so much better—and faster, too, in the long run—to bring the dog along slowly in the first place.

Finally, the signal you give your assistant should be quite different from the signals you give your dog. If it is not, and you have to handle your dog before the dummy is thrown, you will probably get dummies thrown when you don't want them, and at times when your temper is flaring. Many good training teams have been broken up over a few incidents like that. Make the signal you give your assistant quite distinct. I wave my hat back and forth a few times to signal my assistant.

MISSING-THE-POINT BLIND

In the test shown in Figure 57, the bird is planted in open water out past a tempting point of land. The point is covered with high, dense cover, so if your dog lands there you will not be able to see him, and vice versa. Handling the dog back into the water will

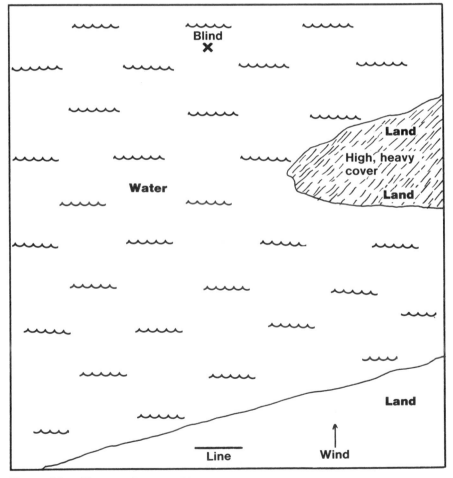

Figure 57. Missing-the-point blind.

be very difficult, if not impossible. For these reasons, the dog has to stay off that point of land.

Before sending your dog, you can do two things to prevent the dog from landing on the point.

First, you can "No" the dog off the point. You do this by sitting the dog at heel facing the point and then saying "No." The dog that is well trained in what "No" means will avoid any place you "No" him away from. The training for this involves going through this "No" process and then correcting the dog as he lands if he heads for the point. The correction should not come until he lands, to take advantage of the dog's place consciousness. Again, you should talk with a competent professional to learn how to correct under these circumstances. The necessary correction is too intricate to learn from a book.

The second measure you can take—as you might have guessed by now—is to lead the dog a little to the left of the bird. If he turns toward the point, you will have room to handle him away. If not, you can handle him to the bird as he swims. You will handle him away from the point only in field trials and while hunting; if he heads for the point during training—and if you have "No-ed" him away from it before you sent him—let him reach land and then correct him—every time. In training, the emphasis is on training the dog; in field trials and hunting, it is on retrieving the bird. Handle in the latter situations; correct in the former.

GETTING-THE-POINT BLIND

For years field trial judges set up missing-the-point blinds—those that tempt the dog to take a little juke and hunt on land when the blind was actually in water. Trainers worked hard to convince their dogs that those islands and points of land were forbidden. Then one judge said to another, "I wonder what would happen if we set up a test in which the dogs were supposed to land on a point and drive on through it?" Not too surprisingly, many dogs refused to land and swam around the point, ignoring their handlers' whistles. These dogs had been convinced that all sorts of bad things would happen to them if they landed in such a place, so they simply refused to do so. This test gave judges a new way to eliminate dogs when they really needed to, and it gave trainers a new dimension to their water blind problems.

This may seem like a contrived test for advanced field trial dogs, but one could make a case for its applicability to a hunting

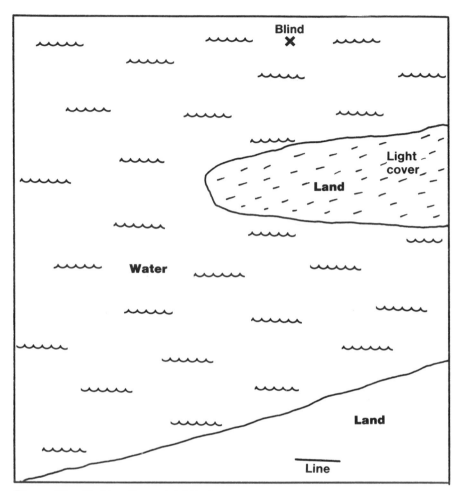

Figure 58. Getting-the-point blind.

situation. What if there were a barbed-wire fence under the sur-
face of the water off the point? It would then be dangerous for a
dog to swim around the point; across it would be the only way you
could send your dog. Once again, we are talking about control.
The dog that can be sent over the point on one test and kept away
from it on the next, or vice versa, is under better control than the
dog that always goes on land or never does so.

    The dog that has not been trained to avoid the point in the
missing-the-point test will not have any trouble with this one. This
test is really a trap for the dog that has been overtrained to stay in
the water on water blinds. As a trainer you must strive for balance
in your water-forcing. You must be able to line your dog past the
point when necessary and also to line him across it when that is
required. If you cue the dog a little, he will be able to figure out
which is expected when. When the dog is to stay off the point, you
should "No" him away from it before you send him. When you

want him to cross it, you should not "No" him off it. Given enough of this training, the dog will learn what you expect of him. This training won't happen quickly, and you will face a number of difficulties, but you and your dog will succeed if you train consistently.

CHANNEL BLIND

Figure 59 shows the famous—or infamous—channel blind. Many newcomers to field trials see such tests in places where the need to have the dog swim down the channel instead of running the bank is not obvious, and they conclude that field trials are highly artificial affairs. In this diagram you can see two good rea-

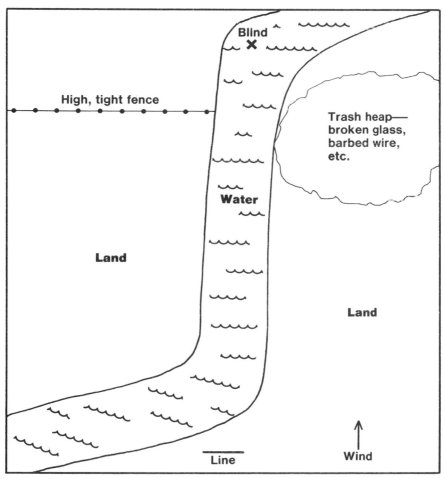

Figure 59. Channel blind.

sons for having the dog stay in the water for the entire retrieve. On one side of the channel is a high, tight fence that the dog cannot pass through; on the other side is a junk pile in which the dog might be injured. In actual hunting, many other obstacles could necessitate keeping the dog in the water: cactus patches, quicksand, high cover in which the dog could not be handled. Unfortunately, on the trial grounds where field trial judges have to test this kind of control, such obstacles usually don't exist, and so the judges have to set up such tests without the hazards shown here. Experienced participants and spectators can imagine hazards around the test areas even if the dangers aren't really there, because field trial people know what the judges are looking for and understand the limits of the trial grounds. Newcomers, however, are likely to damn the test, the judges, and field trials in general.

Field trials aren't perfect—what is?—but they do a fairly good job of determining which dogs are most satisfactory as hunting companions. In this test, for example, which dog would you rather hunt with, the one that can stay in the water and retrieve the bird or the dog that will not stay off the shore, fails to retrieve the bird, and maybe even gets hurt during the test?

It all boils down to control over the dog. Either you have it or you don't. The handler who can keep a dog in the water on a channel blind has control; the handler who can't, doesn't.

The training for this test is similar to that for keeping a dog off a point of land. "No" him off both shores and then correct him as soon as he lands on either side. If the channel is shallow enough, it is a good idea to start out in the water, close to the blind, and slowly work back away from the fall. I don't know any handlers who have fully trained their retrievers without getting wet themselves—and rather often at that. If you start out in the water and close to the blind your dog is far less likely to refuse to enter the water when you say "Back" than he would be if you had started with the full-length channel blind and a lot of correction every time he landed. Lead him through this test until he understands what you want before you start correcting him for "disobedience."

MINIATURE CHANNEL BLIND

The test shown in Figure 60 is in many ways tougher than the channel blind. Here the dog has to run quite a distance on land before he reaches the water. Then he comes to a narrow point of water surrounded by land. He will see that veering just

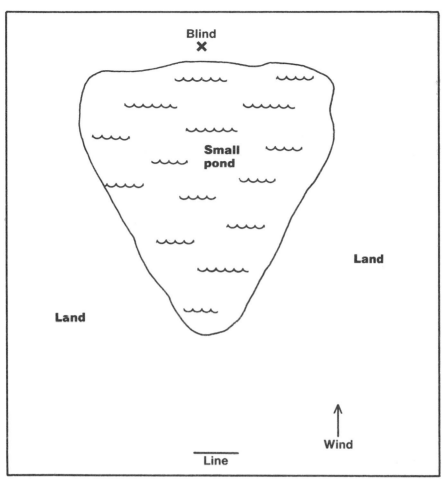

Figure 60. Miniature channel blind.

slightly and staying on land would be much easier than swimming all the way to the bird.

As the test is here diagrammed, there is no apparent reason for sending the dog through the water to retrieve this bird. It would be much simpler and faster to send him around. However, you can imagine situations in which the dog would have to go through the water or not complete the test. The terrain in Figure 59 is one example. Since such situations exist, it is a good idea to train your dog to stay in the water when you tell him to do so.

To train for this test, start either in the water or right at the water's edge, depending on how deep the pond is at the point. Convince your dog that this is the way you want him to do the test—in the water. Placing the bird in the water also helps. That way the dog never needs to land during the test.

Once he is doing good work from the edge of the water, back

up slowly and try him from spots that are farther and farther away from the point. Eventually, he will decide to go around the point, of course, but that won't be until after he fully understands what you expect of him. When he does go around, correct him, but be careful where you do it. Let him run about halfway around the pond first. If you correct him anywhere near the place where he is supposed to enter the water—or even worse, between the line and the water—you will be training him to refuse to leave when you say "Back." That is certain to cause a serious problem. Wait until he reaches a place he shouldn't be in before you correct him. He will avoid that place on repeat runs of the test. Remember that dogs are place conscious.

NO-PICTURE BLIND

In Figure 61 we see a blind that is designed to prevent the dog from forming a mental picture of the situation before he is sent from the line to retrieve. A dike directly in front of the line prevents the dog from seeing the water, much less forming a picture. After the dog has gone over the dike, the handler is allowed to climb to the top of it to handle the dog.

In my frequently erroneous opinion, this is a totally contrived test. It has no application to hunting, for there the handler would take the dog to the top of the dike before sending him. Why not? He has to handle from there anyway. Most advanced, or difficult, field trial tests have a basis in hunting—a tenuous one, perhaps, but a basis nonetheless. The no-picture blind, however, is purely a field trial aberration with no reason for existence other than to force the dog to go to the edge of the water with no plan of attack for the retrieve he must attempt.

This test reminds me of a ridiculous drill we used to have to go through in baseball when I was a kid. The coach would hit a ball to an outfielder and at the exact moment when it hit the glove, would tell him where to throw it. Any outfielder who has played the game at all plans where he will throw the ball before the pitch is made: a hit in front of him will go to second (can't throw the runner out at third); a hit behind him will go to the cutoff man; a short fly will go home to get the runner at third; a long fly will go to the cutoff man, and so forth. Each batter coming to the plate requires the outfielders to plan where they will throw, but never do they wait until the ball is in the glove to make these decisions.

That ridiculous drill was used only in practice, but the no-picture blind sometimes appears in the "game," the field trial.

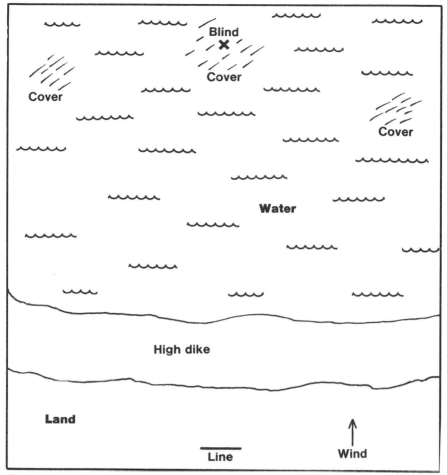

Figure 61. No-picture blind.

I recommend that you not even bother with this test until you are into advanced field trial work and you know that some of the judges you will compete under are likely to spring a no-picture blind. When you reach that point, you will have enough experience to devise ways in which to train for it. Naturally, your initial training will involve running your dog on pattern blinds that simulate this test. The simplest way to start this training is to plant large white plastic dummies, which are highly visible. The dog will gradually learn to find a mental picture quickly when he first sees the water. At that point, this test changes from a no-picture blind to a late-picture blind. Even then, it is highly contrived.

5. SUCTION BLIND RETRIEVES

Training Tips

This chapter deals with the more advanced blind retrieves, those in which some element is introduced to attract the dog away from the line his handler has given him to the blind. There are several forms of this suction: other blinds in the same test, other marks in the same test, fired shots, decoys, and so forth. Each is treated in this chapter.

All of these forms of suction are used routinely in all-age stakes at field trials. All are part of a typical day's hunt in which blind retrieves are necessary. Consequently, if you have either field trial or hunting aspirations for your dog, you should train him to ignore these suction devices when doing blind retrieves.

Such training is relatively simple. You introduce the suction device into the dog's pattern blinds first. Then you use it on reruns only in regular blind retrieves. Finally, you use it in regular blinds. This method sounds simple, and it is, but it isn't quick. If you attempt to rush through these three steps too rapidly, you will spend most of your time going back to the first step—starting all over again. Take your time with this training, and it won't take forever; rush it, and it just might.

Throughout this training, it is important that your dog understand what you mean when you "No" him off a suction factor. From the first time you introduce one into his pattern blinds, you should form the habit of sitting him facing the suction device and saying "No" just before you set him up for the blind. That won't mean much to him until he makes a mistake and gets corrected for sucking back to the place you have "No-ed" him away from. If you will let him get all the way there before you correct him—

126

Figure 62.   A golden retriever brings a duck back through decoys. Decoys can be used as a suction device in blind retrieves.

much as you did in correcting him for switching—he will soon learn that your "No" has real authority.

Use a softly spoken "No" for this. Your dog can be trained to respond as well to this as to a bellowed "No," and you will not spook as many ducks when you have to use this technique in hunting. If you insist that your dog do the work your way or suffer the consequences—every time—he will respond to a quiet "No." If you let him get away with sucking back sometimes, all the bellowing in the world will not control him.

If two suction devices appear in a test—such as a double mark along with the blind—"No" your dog away from each individually before you send him for the blind.

Once your dog is thoroughly trained on suction blinds, you will not have to "No" him every time, as you did through the early stages of his training. He will come to understand that he is to stay away from old falls, old blinds, decoys, and so forth when you line him in a different direction. Even an old dog will sometimes become too interested in one of these distractions, however, and the training he has had in being "No-ed" away from problems comes in handy on those occasions. If you understand your dog as you should, you will be able to tell when to "No" him and when a suction device presents no real problem to him. Here we are talking about the well-trained dog; the beginner should be "No-ed" every time, even if he looks as if he doesn't need it. He is being trained in what "No" means, so he needs to hear it every time.

These few tips do not, of course, constitute a complete training program for suction blinds. I doubt if one exists, for every time you think you are doing well, some judge invents a new test to prove that you aren't.

Handling Techniques

HUNTING SITUATIONS

The basic rules for handling a dog to a suction blind are the same as those that apply to a simple blind: know where the wind is coming from, give your dog an appropriate initial line, and handle calmly as you do in training—even if the first Canada goose you ever shot is at stake. In addition, you will have to be able to "No" your dog away from old marks and other hazards. These may include a dead duck right in the middle of the decoys in a situation where a lively cripple is about to get away and you want your dog to retrieve it first and leave the easy dead bird for later. If your dog didn't see the cripple fall, this is a blind retrieve. If he did see the dead one fall among the decoys, it is a difficult suction blind. Either you will succeed when you "No" him away from the dead duck or you will probably lose the cripple—and this is not an uncommon occurrence in duck hunting over decoys. Many cripples are lost every year because most handlers cannot successfully "No" their dogs away from the easy dead mark.

A suction blind can occur in the uplands, too. While hunting pheasant, for example, you might shoot two birds, but your dog might see only the first one because he was chasing it when the second one flushed. If you handle this as a blind rather than as a "Hunt 'em out" retrieve, it will be a suction blind because the dog will tend to be drawn back to the fall he has already retrieved. If there is not a stream or some other obstacle in the way, I tend to use "hot pursuit" and "Hunt 'em out" on falls of this type. Still, if an obstacle is present, this must be handled as a suction blind, and it is a tough one.

In all these suction blinds, set your dog up facing the suction problem, "No" him away from it and set him up once more facing the blind. Then go through your usual blind retrieve sequence:

Figure 63.   A golden with a rooster pheasant.

"Dead bird . . . Line . . . Back!"— or whatever commands you use.
Try to give your dog time to form a picture of the situation before
you send him. This is difficult because the bird might be a cripple
and you want to send the dog to it as soon as possible. Sometimes
you make better time if you don't hurry too much, however.

FIELD TRIAL HANDLING

If you are less than absolutely certain that your dog will take
and hold the line you give him without being pulled back to old
falls or hazards, you should "No" him away from them before you
start your blind retrieve sequence. Sit him facing the hazard, let
him look at it, and command "No" as sharply as the dog requires.
If there are two hazards, as in a double mark with a blind between
them, "No" him off both of them.

Of course, the dog first has to be trained to understand what

Figure 64. A double mark with a double blind. The judge is signalling to the right-hand guns while the dog and handler watch attentively. The left-hand guns are going to shoot a flier, as can be seen from the fact that there is more than one shooter. The blinds are marked by the two stakes in the ground, one in the middle and the other on the right edge of the picture. The stakes are a fluorescent red, which the handlers can see but which are invisible to the dogs (which are color blind).

"No" means. The technique for teaching "No" was covered earlier in this chapter. Suffice it to say here that the "No" command is the basis for teaching your dog to understand and handle suction blinds. Initially you will "No" him away from every hazard in every such test. As he becomes more familiar with suction blinds, you will not find it necessary to "No" him off the hazards every time. You will be able to tell by his actions at the line whether or not a hazard is distracting him. If he appears to be having trouble with one, then you should "No" him away from it. If he seems to understand that he is to avoid the hazard, then you can ignore it. When in doubt, always "No" him just to be safe. This is just another part of the teamwork between you and your dog that makes retriever training and handling so challenging.

If you train him with quiet "No" commands, he will respond to them in a trial. If you shout in training, you will have to shout in trials. Which do you think is more appropriate?

Some handlers give their dogs a hand signal as they "No" them away from a hazard just as they do when they give them the line to the blind. Others believe that the hand should always point out the right direction and hence should be used only when giving a line to the blind. I have seen top professionals do it both ways, so it seems to be a matter of preference more than anything else. Whichever way you do it, however, be consistent.

In training, if your dog veers off toward the hazard after initially heading toward the blind, let him go all the way to the hazard before you correct him. That way you can take advantage of his place consciousness as it relates to correction.

If the dog veers off during a trial, handle him as quickly as possible. It normally is not too good an idea to try an angled "Back" to help him out of trouble; a soft "Over" is probably the surest way, followed by a straight "Back." You have to know your dog. The fact that he is being drawn toward the hazard indicates that you should be conservative in selecting your cast. When in doubt, use the soft "Over" away from the hazard and then a straight "Back" when the dog is once again on track.

On land, it is a good idea to let your dog sit and look at you a second or two before you give him the cast. You cannot do this in water, of course, because the dog cannot stay still there. The reason for doing this when you can is to let him get the hazard off his mind a little before you try to handle him away from it. Let him sit there for a moment and think about what you are about to do before you do it. Here again, remember that no prize is given to the fastest handler in the trial. Take your time, and you'll get better work out of your dog.

Unexpected hazards sometimes pop up during a trial, and you will have to handle your dog away from them quickly. I have many times seen a wild pheasant flush in front of a dog unexpectedly. Never mind that dogs had been running along the same line all day without a bird flushing. Pheasants are unpredictable. When this happens to you, you must handle quickly if your dog looks as if he wants to chase the bird into the next county. The sooner you stop him, the better are your chances of keeping him out of trouble.

Once when I was running Duffy in a licensed trial, we were almost done in by a butterfly! I had stopped Duffy with the whistle, and just as I gave him an "Over," a butterfly flew up in front of his nose. Duffy ignored my cast, jumped up after the butterfly, and started chasing it. Fortunately, I was able to stop him with the whistle again and handle him successfully, without further interference from the butterfly. As he picked up the bird, I turned to the judges and said, "That little incident with the butterfly really wasn't the dog's fault. You see, I could never afford to buy birds to train him with, so I had to use butterflies." They both laughed, and I think they wanted to give me an award for the most original excuse they had heard all day.

Training Tests

The rest of this chapter is devoted to diagrams and explanations of suction blind retrieve training tests. Only artificial suction factors are treated here: dry guns, old falls, and so forth. Cover, terrain, and wind factors are covered in Chapter 4, "Basic Blind Retrieves." Only in those instances where natural factors create a special problem in a suction blind are they discussed in this chapter.

I accidentally created a suction problem with Duffy when he was young, and it took a considerable amount of work by a good pro, Jim Robinson, to solve the problem. I created it by using the "thrown blind" technique, which is discussed in the out-to-sea blind test (Chapter 4, Figure 56). This is a good technique for water blinds because it allows you to put a blind where you want it without having it drift away before the dog reaches it. The thrown blind can also be used as a positive motivator for the dog: he gets to see the dummy thrown once he swims out far enough. It is not a good technique on land, however, because the dummy usually falls into cover and the dog has to hunt for it. In Duffy's case, I made the mistake of not having my blind thrower hide. Duffy was able to see the thrower from the line before I sent him. Later, when I tried to mix marked retrieves with blinds, Duffy thought that the guns for the marks were going to throw a blind for him. He would head for the guns as soon as I sent him for the blind, no matter where I tried to line him. As I said, Jim Robinson put in quite a bit of effort to cure Duffy of this habit. Had I kept my blind throwers hidden, this problem would never have developed.

Since then, I have had the blind throwers hide so that the dogs cannot see them from the line or from any point on the way out or back. The dummy appears to the dog to fall like manna from heaven when it is thrown. I have not had a serious suction problem since.

DOUBLE BLIND

Figure 65 illustrates the double blind, which can be run on land or in water; it is a basic suction test. Since everyone uses three- or five-spoke pattern blind setups, this is a natural type of suction test to start with. By the time the dog is actually doing blind retrieves, he will have had a lot of experience with this kind of exercise on the pattern field.

Normally, the short blind is retrieved first. The reason for this is that many dogs will pop on the long one after picking up the short one. They seem to expect both birds to be about the same distance from the line. When the dog doesn't find the second one at about that distance, he decides to sit down and talk it over with the handler. The rerun is probably the best cure for this. Rerun your dog two or three times on each of these tests you set up; that way, your dog will come to expect the second blind to be longer than the first. Remember that blind retrieves are memory tests to a far greater extent than we realize. Fill your dog's memory with the right pictures by rerunning him two or three times on those tests that you want him to be able to recall at a field trial or in actual hunting.

Naturally, the second bird should not always be farther from the line than the first. (In retriever training, "always" and "never" are "seldom" appropriate.) Sometimes the birds should be the same distance away, and occasionally, but not too often, the first blind should be the long one. Actually, if you never run it this way, no real harm will result, for it is far easier to handle a dog back in close when he wants to drive too deep than it is the other

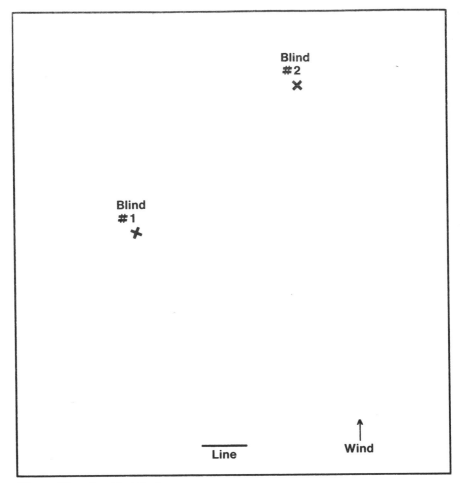

Figure 65. Double blind.

way around. Still, it doesn't hurt to reverse the patterns on occasion.

Naturally, you should "No" your dog away from the line to the first blind before you give him the line to the second one. Help him all you can.

DRY GUN BLIND

A dry gun is a fairly strong form of suction. In it a person stands in a spot that might be used for a mark and fires a shotgun just before the handler sends the dog on a blind retrieve. If the dog is fooled into thinking that the shot was a mark he didn't see, he is likely to run straight to the dry gun when sent. That, of course, is a mistake; the dog is supposed to take the line given him by his handler.

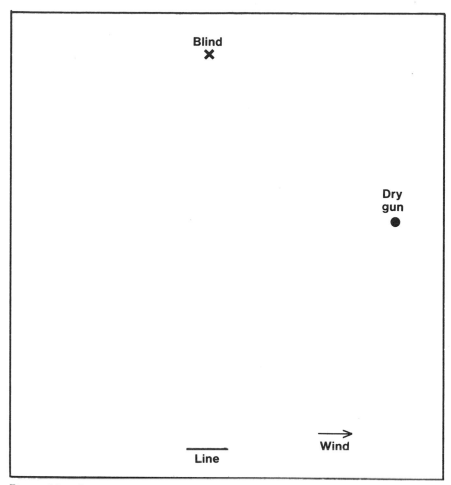

Blind
✗

**Dry
gun**
●

———————
Line

——————▶
Wind

Figure 66.   Dry gun blind.

In handling a dog in a test like the one shown in Figure 66, it is advisable to "No" him away from the dry gun right after the shot and before you give him the line to the blind. That should clear up any doubt in his mind as to whether there is a mark out there. (Most dogs, by the time they are this far along in training, will have picked up many marks that they didn't see fall for one reason or another.)

In the test diagrammed, the wind is blowing toward the dry gun. This will increase the dog's tendency to be drawn in that direction. In fact, he would probably drift that way with the wind even if there were no dry gun out there. For this reason, you must lead him into the wind, as has already been covered.

The initial training for this test should be on the pattern field. Put a dry gun out there while your dog is going through the pattern blind drills. Then, when you want to try the dog on a real blind with a dry gun, use the dry gun only on reruns for a while. If you make everything as gradual and natural as possible, you will save time. If you rush things, you will be forever starting over.

SCENTED POINT BLIND

The test shown in Figure 67 is one in which the dog is expected to swim past a point of land on his way to a water blind. The handler has made the point more tempting by spreading duck or pheasant scent all over it and by making certain that the wind is blowing from the point to the dog as he goes by. Many people regard this as an artificial test designed by field trial judges to confuse and confound retrievers. Maybe so, but do we really know

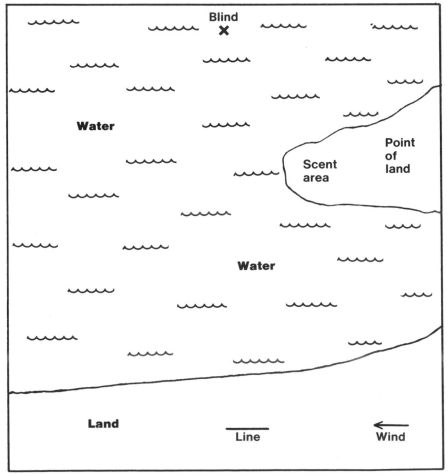

Figure 67.   Scented point blind.

what scents the dog will encounter when sent for a blind retrieve while actually hunting?

During a training session several years ago I was working Brandy on a water blind in which he had to swim past a point of land like this one. I sent him out the first time and stood at the line watching him swim. I glanced at the point when he was still about 50 yards from it, and I could hardly believe what I saw. Three rooster pheasants were strutting around on the point! Frankly, I didn't know what to do. Fortunately, the birds saw Brandy before he saw them, and they slinked off into the cover. Still, the dog got a noseful of them as he went by, and he turned—naturally—to go after them. (Dogs do use their noses, even on blind retrieves.) It took two or three whistles and "Overs" to convince Brandy that I didn't want him to go after those pheasants.

Here again we are talking about the control that is necessary in handling retrievers. In an actual hunting situation, the dog that cannot be kept on line to a blind retrieve when he smells live game (which he couldn't catch anyway) is not as good as the dog that can be so controlled. We want the dog to use his nose, of course, but the handler must have veto power.

In training for this test, use the scent only on reruns for quite a while. Also, "No" your dog away from the point before you give him the line to the blind.

WATER BLIND WITH DECOY

Figure 68 illustrates a cross-channel blind with a single decoy (preferably with a lot of white on it) as a suction device. The decoy is set out in the water directly across the channel from the line. The blind is at an angle across the channel.

Dogs are taught in their marking tests to leave decoys alone. Several decoys are usually set out for this training, however. In this test a single highly visible decoy is used, and it is amazing how this can fool the most decoy-proof dogs. If you put out a dozen blocks, the dogs will ignore them, especially if they are mallard decoys. Put one pintail, whistler, bluebill, or canvasback drake there, however, and the dogs will not be able to get it out of their minds. It must be a real duck, they seem to say to themselves; it has to be.

In running your dog on a test like this, show him the decoy first and then "No" him away from it before giving him the line to the blind.

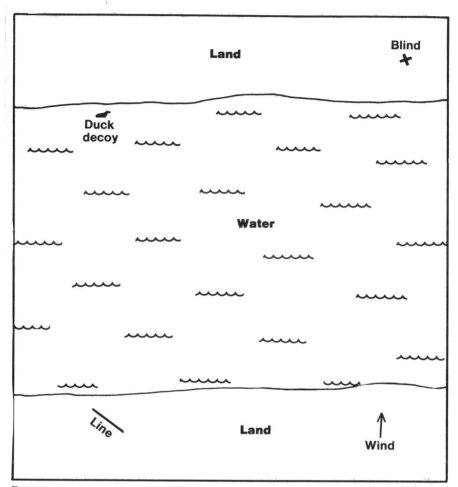

Figure 68. Water blind with decoy.

In training, put the block out only for reruns for a while. Be sure to use a decoy with plenty of white on it; a mallard is too dark to be effective.

Another trick for training on this test is to work on bare ground at first. Here you can correct a dog that runs halfway to the blind and then decides that he just has to check out that single duck over there. If he decides to try this in water, you are pretty limited in what you can do.

This single decoy hazard can be used in many water blinds. Put the decoy where you don't want your dog to go: near the point he has to stay away from, on the shore that he is not supposed to run along, and so forth. Introduce this hazard gradually, however. Use the decoy only as an extra temptation after the dog understands what you want him to do.

COMBINATION SINGLE MARK AND BLIND(S)

In the test shown in Figure 69, the single mark is picked up first, followed by one or both of the blinds. The blinds may be at different distances from the line and closer to or farther from the mark. Of course, this test can be run on land or in water.

The basic purpose of the test is to determine whether or not the dog will suck back to the mark when sent for the blinds.

With wind 69–B (straight downwind from the line), this is a fairly simple test.

With wind 69–A (right to left) and blind M, however, a scent problem arises. Scent from the mark will drift to the dog as he

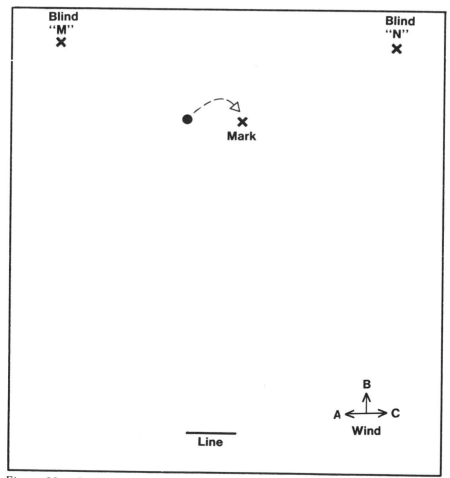

Figure 69.   Combination single mark and blind(s).

goes out for blind M. This is therefore not a good test for young, inexperienced dogs, but it can be used for older, thoroughly trained dogs.

With wind 69–C and blind M a lead problem can develop. This wind tends to blow the dog into the mark as he goes out. Therefore, in order to compensate, the handler has to give the dog a false line to the left of the true line to the blind.

With blind N and winds A and C, the reverse is true.

Training for this test should start on the pattern field. After the dog is comfortable with mixed marks and pattern blinds, he should be given marks on reruns of blinds for a while before trying the test as diagrammed.

If, after all the preliminary training on the pattern field and on reruns, the dog sucks back to the mark on this test when it is run in its entirety, he should be corrected only in the area of the fall (mark), not on the way to it. Once again, remember to correct him where you don't want him to be, so that he will avoid that place. If you correct him on the way there, he will run uncertainly on blinds and maybe even on marks. After a while he may refuse to go at all when you send him. If that happens, you need the help of a professional trainer. You should therefore avoid all these problems by correcting your dog in the appropriate place.

COMBINATION DOUBLE MARK AND BLIND(S)

Figure 70 shows a double mark and the three possible blinds that can be run with it. This can be any double covered in Chapter 2, "Double Marked Retrieves." It can be wide or narrow, short or long. Normally, the blinds are longer than the marks in this kind of test.

The most common double-and-blind test is the wide double with the blind through the middle. This provides double suction. Normally, it is run with wind 70–B (straight downwind). This tests whether the dog will suck back to either mark when sent for the blind. With wind A or C a scent problem can arise from one bird or the other. This is all right for older, more experienced dogs but should be avoided in the early stages of training.

Blinds M and O are similar to the blinds with the single mark. They are included here only to demonstrate that the blind does not have to be in the middle in a double-and-blind test.

Of course, you can use two or three blinds with the marks. Then suction arises from blinds as well as from marks as the dog

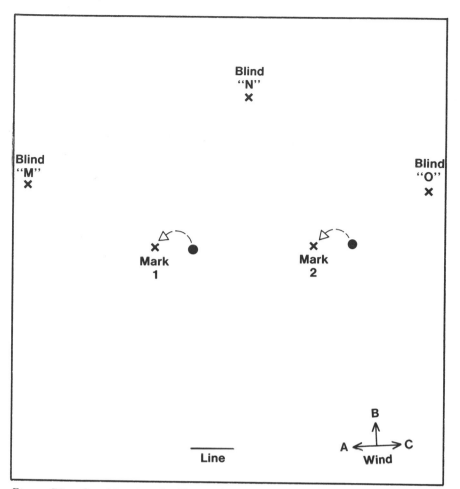

Figure 70. Combination double mark and blind(s).

works his way through the test. Save this for dogs that are quite far along in their training.

Training for this test starts on the pattern field and then continues on reruns only (put the marks in for reruns of the blinds) until the dog is comfortable with the work. Then try the entire test, keeping it simple at first. Any correction for sucking back to a mark should, of course, occur only in the area of the mark.

COMBINATION TRIPLE MARK AND BLIND(S)

A triple mark and all the possible locations for blinds with it are shown in Figure 71. One, two, three, or four blinds may be run with the marks, and this test may be used either on land or in

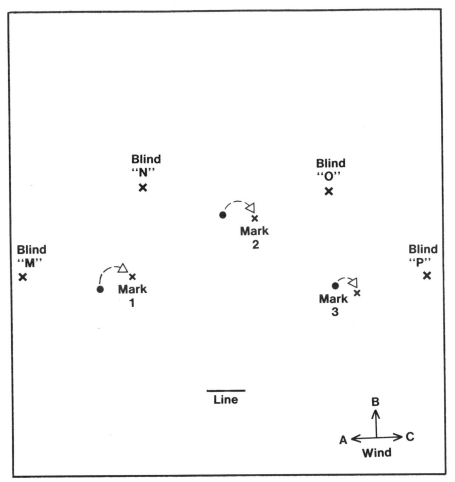

Figure 71. Combination triple mark and blind(s).

water. Sometimes one blind will be picked up before the marks and the other one or two blinds after the mark. You can set up so many tests from this combination—by varying the terrain and cover, the location and sequence of the marks, and the positions of the blinds—that no book could possibly cover them all. Even if it could, as soon as such a book appeared, someone would dream up a new test.

The important thing is to see and understand the basic pattern that underlies all these tests—the pattern that is illustrated here.

Some of the most difficult tests involve running the marks all by themselves first and then coming back thirty minutes or an hour later and running the blind(s). I call this delayed suction. It works especially well if there was an honor on the marks. The honoring dog sees three marks fall and then is taken off line before he sees even one of them picked up. Later he is brought back to the same line and sent for a blind retrieve. If he still remembers those marks, you will have difficulty keeping him from sucking back to them.

You can use delayed suction on any combination test— single, double, or triple marks, with any number of blinds. For many dogs this is more tempting than the standard combination tests.

REVERSE SUCTION

It should come as no surprise to you by now that, if marks can be used to create suction on blind retrieves, blinds can also be used to create suction on marked retrieves. This can be done, and it is, especially in the advanced stakes at field trials. The test shown in Figure 72, however, is not for green dogs.

The blind is run first, and the simpler it is, the better. Ideally, the dog should line it, for you want the dog to remember exactly where the blind is.

After the blind is run, the marks are thrown. Notice that the number one guns are very close to the blind. After the throw, they retire behind the hill. Also, notice that the third mark is a flier. Most dogs become excited when they see several guns in one location, for they know that that means there will be a flier. It is difficult for the dogs to concentrate on any other mark when they know that a live bird is about to take off. As a result, many dogs do not mark the number one and two birds very well.

After the flier is down, the dog is sent after it and typically has little trouble finding it since that is the bird he has been concentrating on. Then he is sent after the number two bird, which he didn't see too well but which he can usually pick up fairly easily from the position of the guns.

Finally the dog is sent for the number one bird. He didn't see this one very well, either, and no guns are in sight to help him. On top of that, there is that blind he ran not far away. Many dogs will rerun the blind instead of going to the now forgotten mark. Then it becomes necessary to handle the dog to the mark. Handling to a mark is penalized in field trials, for the dog is expected to pick up the birds he sees fall without any assistance from his handler. These birds are, after all, marked retrieves. Handling a dog to a bird he saw fall is an annoyance when you are hunting and can cause ducks to avoid your area if you are standing up and waving your arms around when they approach.

Train for this test systematically. First, run your dog on the marks two or three times without having the number one guns

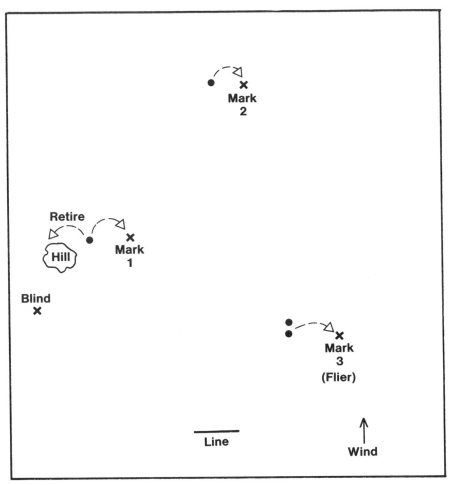

Figure 72.   Reverse suction.

retire. Then run the dog on it perhaps twice with the guns retiring. Then run him on the blind two or three times. Now the dog knows where everything is, so running the test as diagrammed should cause him no problem. Run him on the full test at least twice. Repeat this on several different days in several different places, always starting from scratch. Then try the test with a double mark instead of a triple, and give him the entire test the first time. If he handles it, follow the same procedure in several places over several days before you advance to the triple. If your dog fails to handle the double the first time, go back to the walk-throughs for a while longer.

This procedure involves much running and rerunning for the dog. To ensure the effectiveness of this training, be certain that you do not overwork your dog. Let him rest periodically between reruns; let the training stretch over several training sessions if necessary.

6. GETTING THE MOST FROM YOUR RETRIEVER

What "The Most" Means

We don't have to hunt for food. In fact, if we did, those of us who don't shoot any better than I do would starve.

Since we don't hunt for food, some other reason or set of reasons must explain all the impedimenta, animate and otherwise, that we collect and treasure—guns, field clothes, duck leases, decoys, boats, and most important to many of us, dogs. I could probably shoot as many birds with an old single shot shotgun, but instead I have two high-priced over/unders, and I wouldn't part with either of them. The same is true for all my equipment—and for all of yours. We buy better hunting gear than we need and more than we need, and even so, we feel that our money is well spent. We enjoy our equipment beyond its purely utilitarian value, and we take pride in owning it.

Our dogs are the same, only more so. For much of our hunting, we do not absolutely need them. In fact, many hunters do not use dogs at all—poor souls. Of course, our dogs help us bring in more game and cut our loss of cripples, but if that were all we got out of them, few of us would put up with the expense, inconvenience, and work associated with keeping them twelve months a year.

No, we own dogs because we enjoy having them around, we enjoy doing things with them, and we even enjoy the work they create. Training a dog is one of the greatest pleasures for the true dog lover—even if there are many frustrating days mixed in with the days of genuine accomplishment. Just having a dog sitting in the blind with us can take the disappointment out of a birdless

145

day. During quiet times in the blind, Duffy always insists that I scratch him under the chin. He noses my hand and arm until I do this little service for him without realizing it. Many times, when ducks start to work to my decoys, I find myself blowing the duck call with one hand and unconsciously scratching Duffy's chin with the other.

Dogs are to enjoy.

Unfortunately, many of us do not get all the enjoyment we can for our dog investment, if you will look at it that way for a moment. We train them a little bit, and that's lots of fun; we hunt them as often as we can, but that is not often enough with today's short hunting seasons and low bag limits; we spend time with them around home, which is very enjoyable; and that is about it.

The purpose of this chapter is to suggest a few ways in which you can get more enjoyment from your dog, ways that you possibly have not heard of before—or at least have not seriously considered.

National Breed Clubs

A national breed club sponsors each retriever breed in this country. These clubs are the Labrador Retriever Club of America, the Golden Retriever Club of America, the American Chesapeake Club, The Flat-Coated Retriever Society of America, the Curly-Coated Retriever Club of America, and the Irish Water Spaniel Club of America. Each of these clubs is a member club of the American Kennel Club (AKC). As a matter of fact, every breed recognized by the AKC has a sponsoring national breed club.

You can increase your enjoyment of your dog as well as your knowledge of the breed by joining your national breed club. These clubs offer many valuable services to members.

Most clubs publish a newsletter—monthly, bimonthly, or quarterly—informing members about what is going on in the breed all over the country. Such newsletters also contain educational articles on field, bench, and obedience training. Advertisements for puppies, stud dogs, and equipment are helpful, too. Probably the most significant single feature of these newsletters, however, is the information they contain about proper breeding—how you can improve the breed, how others are trying to do so. If you have any intention of breeding your dog, you should become knowledgeable on the subject first. Even if you have no such intentions, you will probably be in the market for another dog sometime, so you should learn what kind of breeding is going on, what improvements are being sought, and how successful breeders have been in their efforts. The newsletter of your national club will keep you up to date.

National breed clubs sponsor a number of special competitions in field, bench, and obedience. Although these specialties are intended primarily as ways to improve the breed—or at least to measure how well different breeders are doing—they are also enjoyable social events where people interested in the same breed come together from all over the country once a year to become better acquainted and to "talk dogs." At these events you can enjoy the usual rounds of parties, dinners, business meetings, and committee meetings as well as the competitive events: obedience trials, bench shows, and field trials. The "national" offers a chance to see the best dogs from all over the country in one place at one time, and to meet the finest people on earth.

One of the most important functions of the national breed clubs is their sponsorship of the working certificate programs—noncompetitive field trials in which dogs can earn certificates attesting to their ability in the field. The programs were developed to allow bench breeders to prove their breeding stock in the field without expending the time, energy, and money required to compete in field trials. Working certificate tests are much simpler than field trial tests, for the most part, but they do show that a dog has, or does not have, the basic retrieving instincts we expect of the retriever breeds. Because they are noncompetitive, a retriever does not necessarily have to "beat" any other dogs to qualify; all dogs pass or fail on the basis of their own performance. Each national breed club has its own set of requirements for its certificate, which is perhaps unfortunate. It might be better if there were only one set of standards for all retriever breeds. Some clubs have more than one type of certificate, each with its own requirements, with one more difficult than the other. The Golden Retriever Club of America, for example, has a WC and a WCX. The WC (working certificate) requires a fairly simple land double and two back-to-back water singles, while the WCX (Working Certificate Excellent) requires a land triple and a water double. At this time, not one of the national breed clubs requires a blind retrieve for its working certificate. That is unfortunate, too, for the blind retrieve is very important in an ordinary day's shoot for most of us.

Dogs that pass the working certificate tests are given a certificate attesting to that fact and are allowed to carry the appropriate letters after their names: WC, WCX, WD (working dog—Chesapeake Club), and so forth. The presence of these letters in a pedigree gives puppy purchasers some assurance that the ancestors of their puppies had some working ability. These titles do not carry the significance of FC (field champion) or AFC (amateur field champion), of course, but they are important nevertheless.

If you do not plan to pursue the FC or AFC titles, and if you would like to breed your dog someday, you would be wise to join your national breed club and try to earn a working certificate before you do any breeding.

How do you join your national breed club? Write to the American Kennel Club (51 Madison Avenue, New York, N.Y. 10010) and ask for the name and address of the secretary of your national breed club. Then write to the secretary for more information.

Local Breed Clubs

Under the wing of each national breed club are a number of local or regional clubs. The goals of the local clubs are similar to those of the national clubs, except that they are local in nature. The newsletter of the national club usually contains news from each local club affiliated with it.

Membership in these local clubs can be very enjoyable. Although their members are interested in all three major areas of retriever activity—field, bench, and obedience competition—field work will probably have the fewest supporters. Bench and obedience events will dominate the activities of most local clubs, probably because field enthusiasts tend to join local retriever field trial clubs and stay out of the local breed clubs. If more of us would join the local breed clubs, there would be more field activities. Actually, many of these clubs would like to become more active in the field, but they have no members to lead them. Many have tried to start working certificate training programs but have had only marginal success for lack of knowledgeable persons to guide them. Others, with appropriate leadership, have sound programs.

The working certificates offered by the national breed clubs have done much to stimulate the local breed clubs' interest in field activities. If more of us who train working retrievers for field trials and hunting would join these clubs and offer to help the bench and obedience people with their field training programs, the breeds would benefit immeasurably. Some clubs already have well-directed programs, of course, but they could always use more help.

Although I don't believe that membership in a local breed

club is as important as joining the national breed club, I do think that it is well worth the cost, which is usually low. As a member of the local breed club, you will meet people who are interested in the same breed as you are. Perhaps their interest follows a different path—bench or obedience. Still, that is their way of enjoying the breed. If you approach them with an open mind, you may even find new ways of enjoying your own dog. You also might be able to make a genuine contribution to the club by assisting to set up or to perpetuate a field training program for those who are interested but lack the necessary knowledge and experience.

How do you join your local breed club? If there is one in your area, your national breed club secretary will be able to give you the information you need.

Retriever Field Trial Clubs

Retriever field trial clubs sponsor AKC-licensed field trials all over the country. Such a club almost certainly exists in your area. Most of these clubs are organized for people with an interest in any breed of retriever and an interest in field trials or hunting—usually both. A number of activities held by these clubs should be of interest to you.

First, such a club usually leases a piece of land for members to use as a training field. You can never have enough places to train, so if you find two or three such clubs in your area, you will do well to join all of them, if only to gain access to the training grounds.

Second, some field trial clubs conduct training classes for beginners. If you are new to field work, you might find such a class very valuable. Not only will you learn a lot about how to train your own dog, but you will also see that other people's dogs do not always respond exactly as yours does. This will help you when the time comes to start with your second dog: you won't be surprised if this one requires a different approach. The second dog is frequently a disappointment, simply because it is not an exact duplicate of the first. This is especially true for an owner who has had some success with the first dog. Such owners often think that they know all there is to know about retriever training because they did so well with one dog. When the second dog doesn't respond to exactly the same procedures, they feel that something is wrong with the dog, not with the approach. Some people can never successfully train a second dog, no matter how many they start. They have become too inflexible. What worked with old Rex ought to

Figure 73.   A cold-weather fun trial. Some clubs hold fun trials the year around, even when there is a little snow on the ground, as here. One judge is signalling for a bird to be thrown while the handler and dog watch intently.

work with any dog worth training, they think. If you work in a beginners' group, you will see that different dogs respond to different techniques. If you realize this, the initial failures with your second dog will not throw you into a fit of depression.

Local field trial clubs also conduct fun trials frequently, sometimes every month during the spring, summer, and early fall.

A fun trial is really a practice field trial. It is usually a two-day affair held on a Saturday and Sunday, whereas licensed field trials are three-day events because of the big entries. Fun trials include nonregular stakes, in addition to those also held in licensed trials. The regular stakes are the derby (for dogs up to twenty-four months old), the qualifying (for dogs of any age that have not had sufficient wins to be ineligible for this stake), the amateur (for dogs of all ages, as long as they are handled by amateurs and regardless of who trained them), and the open (for dogs of all ages, with no other qualification; this is the *big* stake in which the pros compete). The fun trial nonregular stakes are the puppy stake, for dogs under twelve months old, and the gun dog stake, for dogs of all ages that have not yet placed in the qualifying, amateur, or open stakes.

Competition is high at fun trials, and frequently trophies are awarded to dogs that place in each stake. The entry is small and comprised mostly of local dogs. The big-name professionals who travel the licensed-trial circuit won't be there, although some local pros may participate.

Fun trials will teach you field trial procedures and will give you an idea of how well your training program is working. If your dog does well in training but fails time after time to finish the first series at a fun trial, you might suspect there is a flaw in your training program. You can pinpoint your problem by discussing your program with some of the more knowledgeable members.

A fun trial is also a good warm-up and conditioner for hunting. The dog that has run in a fun trial every month all summer and through the early fall will be ready for hunting when the season opens. This dog will also be in better condition than the dog that has been lying around the house or kennel all that time.

Finally, fun trials are great fun. You gather with other club members and a few visitors from other clubs in the area. You watch good dog work   and bad, sometimes, too. You talk dogs and hunting for the entire weekend. Men, women, and children participate in all events. There is a cook-out on Saturday evening, and some people even camp out all night—and maybe catch fish in the lease lake.

Retriever field trial clubs also sponsor various educational programs, including judges' clinics in which two or three well-known field trial judges conduct a seminar on field trials, dog handling, and judging. These are very enlightening to owners who are interested in improving their performance in field trials or just in understanding dogs better.

These clubs also offer the usual round of social activities—the Christmas party, the annual picnic, and the annual or semiannual business meeting with its social hour, dinner, and entertainment.

The big event for these clubs, however, is the licensed trial. Some clubs hold one every year; others offer two. Holding a licensed trial requires an unbelievable amount of work. Even if the club conducts only one trial annually, planning toward it will go on all year long. Club members must coordinate with the AKC, select judges, correspond with those judges, select a site, find someone to provide birds at a reasonable price, prepare and mail entry forms, and prepare the program. All of this work must be done before the trial starts, an effort that most club members are not even aware of.

During the trial, there is a constant demand for workers: bird throwers, shooters, blind planters, stake marshals, runners to provide food for the judges, and other helpers. Since there are usually two stakes going on all the time, many people are needed to keep the trial going. Ideally, every club member pitches in and helps. If this happens, the trial runs smoothly, and all the people who come from other areas to run their dogs have a good time. Some even comment on the trial's "good mechanics." If the club members do not pitch in, however, delays will result because of the shortage of workers, visitors will have to be asked to help, and the participants will complain about the "bad mechanics" of the trial. Visitors are less likely to come back next year.

After the trial is over, the members who have worked like galley slaves for three days sometimes wonder why they ever joined the club in the first place. They wonder whether holding a licensed trial is worth all the effort. It is, and they know it, but they wonder a little anyhow.

Financially, the licensed trial carries the club. Dues are expected to cover the cost of the leased training grounds and no more. Fun trial entry fees are supposed to cover the expenses of the fun trials themselves, but they frequently fall short. Everything else that the club does depends on profits from the licensed trial. Entries are large, because field trial championship points as well as derby points, national amateur, and national open qualifications are awarded at licensed trials. It is not unusual for sixty to eighty dogs to be entered in the open stake, forty to sixty in the amateur, twenty-five to forty in the qualifying, and thirty to fifty in the derby. At thirty-five dollars an entry the licensed trial brings in a lot of money. Expenses are high, too, but even so, the licensed trial is a money-maker without which most clubs could not survive.

The licensed trial also lets the club reciprocate with other clubs that have held licensed trials. The members of your club go to the other club's trial to relax and enjoy themselves as they run their dogs while the members of the other club work like slaves. Now it is your club's turn to entertain.

The licensed trial also gives all members of the club the opportunity to see top dogs from all over the country in action. The big-name professionals travel from one licensed trial to another, running their strings of dogs in each. Club members who compete in such trials here and there will have an opportunity to see these top pros and their dogs often—too often if they are competing against them. The members who do not participate in licensed trials, however, would never have the opportunity to see the dogs they hear and read about if it weren't for their own club's licensed trial. They sometimes have to watch in uncomfortable circumstances, of course—standing in the rain; throwing dead, soggy pheasants until their arms ache; and wondering whether their bladders will hold up until someone else replaces them. Even so, it is an exciting experience to see these top dogs perform.

The underlying purpose of the licensed trial is to improve the retriever breeds. The dogs that win become the parents of the next generation of field trial retrievers. The real aim of field trials is to help breeders select stock, and these breeders have been so successful in their efforts that the dogs improve measurably from generation to generation. You can infer this from the fact that field trial tests grow harder and harder as time goes by. If dogs were not getting better and better, they could not succeed in these more difficult tests. Actually, better dogs and better training techniques are forcing judges to set up more difficult tests and to raise their expectations. As field trial dogs get better, hunters find it possible to buy better and better hunting dogs—if they buy from the right litters. We all benefit from the long-range results of field trials on the retriever breeds.

As you can see from the number of activities we have mentioned, the retriever field trial club has a great deal to offer. You can participate at whatever level you choose. Some members just use the training grounds to loosen up their dogs before the hunting season each year. Others take advantage of the training classes and the social activities. Still others become involved in the fun trials and maybe participate in a licensed trial now and then. Finally, there are those who completely lose their minds over the sport and run their dogs in licensed trials twenty-five to thirty times a year. You can choose your own level of involvement, based on your interests, your time and money limitations, and the abilities of your dog(s).

Unfortunately, not many dog owners are able to run a great number of licensed trials every year. The time and money required are beyond most of us. With each entry costing thirty-five dollars and with multiple entries the norm (amateur and open, for example), a person can spend a lot just in entry fees by running twenty-five or thirty trials a year. Then there are traveling expenses—gas, oil, lodging, meals, and that always-larger-than-expected "miscellaneous." Some save on lodgings and meals by traveling in campers or motor homes, but they pay more for gas and oil, and they have to pay for the vehicles and for the higher maintenance required.

Then there are training expenses. Many of the really dedicated licensed trialers have their dogs with a pro full-time, twelve months a year. That is very expensive. Even if you choose not to do that, you will be competing against these dogs in every trial, so you will have to find some way to compensate. Normally this means training harder and more often yourself, plus occasionally using a pro to help you over a rough spot. Training every day is not cheap, considering the cost of gas and oil, birds, leases on land, and so forth.

Any way you look at it, serious field trialing is expensive. It also takes more time than most of us can devote to a hobby. Each licensed trial is a three-day affair—Friday, Saturday, and Sunday. Typically, the open and qualifying stakes will be run on Friday and Saturday while the amateur and the derby will run on Saturday and Sunday. That means that if you are running a dog in the open and the amateur, as many do, you will be there from 8:00 A.M. Friday until Sunday afternoon. If the trial is very far from your home, you will need Thursday and possibly Monday to travel. Not many of us can take time off from work from Thursday through Monday

Figure 74. Jumping is required in advanced Obedience Classes. Here Obedience Trial Champion Meadowpond Tackle clears the bar jump. Photo by Cherie Berger.

for twenty-five or thirty weeks a year, even if we can afford all the other costs of the trials. Those who can afford a full-time pro trainer often let the pro run their dogs in the open and will arrive on Saturday to run the amateur themselves.

For those who can afford it, running licensed field trials is a great sport. Unfortunately, most of us have neither the time nor the money to participate seriously.

Still, many of us can afford to run two or three licensed trials each spring and two or three more in the fall. Those who compete on such a limited basis will not have much of a chance to win an FC or an AFC, but they can have a great deal of fun and achieve some lesser goals such as having a dog become a "qualified all-age dog," which requires a first or second place in the qualifying stake or a placement or jam in the open or amateur. This is a significant achievement and one that is within the capabilities of those who can run only a few trials a year.

Participating in a few licensed trials a year and running in several fun trials will give you some fine opportunities to enjoy your retriever. You can do your own training, but that will not be cheap at this level, for you will have to train almost every day if you hope to keep your dog sharp enough for licensed trial competition. Frequent participation in fun trials will keep your handling sharp as well as keep your dog used to working around crowds and among other dogs. This level of competition will also give you a hunting dog that will be the envy of everyone you share a blind with.

Obedience Trial Clubs

Although you may have all you can handle with the national breed club, the local breed club, and the local retriever field trial club, you should at least know about a couple of other clubs.

The AKC sponsors obedience trials for all breeds. The format for these trials is worth a little study. Three progressive obedience titles can be earned in a noncompetitive manner: CD (Companion Dog), CDX (Companion Dog Excellent), and UD (Utility Dog). Classes for dogs seeking each of these titles are held at every obedience trial: the novice classes for the CD., the open classes for the CDX, and the utility classes for the UD. To gain a title, a dog must earn three qualifying scores under three different judges at three separate obedience trials. To be entered in the open classes a dog must have already earned the CD in the novice classes. Before being entered in the utility classes, he must have already earned the CDX in the open classes.

There is no competition for the three titles. All dogs either pass or fail on their own performance. They do not have to beat any other dogs to earn a "leg" toward the title. Placements are awarded and prizes given to the dogs that earn the top four scores in each class and to the highest scoring dog in the trial. Thus there is an element of competition in these trials, and for those seeking placements, the competition is keen. For those who just want their dogs to earn the titles, however, no competition is required. The dogs simply have to pass with the required scores.

Figure 75. Golden retrievers competing in a conformation dog show. The handlers are moving their dogs for the judge (not in picture) to see. Good movement is considered very important in all the sporting breeds.

Another level of competition is available to those who wish it. After earning the UD, a dog can continue to enter trials and compete for championship points, and these points are awarded on a purely competitive basis. After earning the required number of points, a dog is given the title Obedience Trial Champion, which is similar to Field Trial Champion.

As you can see, those who are interested in obedience trials can choose whatever level of competition they wish, set appropriate goals, and become as involved as they wish.

Retrievers do well in obedience trials. Actually, only a little polishing is needed to prepare the typical field trial retriever for the novice classes in obedience trials. The open and utility classes are much more advanced, of course, but the novice classes are well within the ability of most field trial retrievers—if the handlers will insist on more precision than is usually seen in their dogs' responses to basic obedience commands.

Clubs conduct AKC obedience trials in almost every medium- and large-sized city in the country. They also typically conduct beginners' training classes, in which new members can learn how to teach their dogs basic obedience. The average beginning field trainer would do well to take his or her dog through one of these classes. The obedience trial club knows obedience better than does the field trial club, believe me. Information about obedience clubs in your area can be obtained from the AKC.

Dog Shows

Another highly competitive activity pursued by some retriever owners is competing in dog shows, often called bench or conformation shows. These are sponsored by the AKC, and they are for all AKC-recognized breeds. Their purpose is to improve the breeds by awarding championship points to the dogs of each breed that most closely conform to the written standard of physical perfection for that breed. In a sense, they are beauty contests for dogs, and they appear as such to the uninitiated. Actually, conformation to the standard, not "beauty" is rewarded, however.

In these shows, dogs first compete within their own breeds for championship points and best-of-breed ribbons. Then the best dog of each breed is judged in the appropriate group—Sporting, Hound, Working, Terrier, Toy, and Non-sporting. The winners of the six groups are then judged together, and one is chosen as Best in Show.

Championship points are awarded in the breed judging. A dog must win fifteen points to become a Champion. Those points must be won under three different judges and must include at least two majors—wins of three, four, or five points—under at least two different judges. The number of points awarded in each breed at each show is based on the number of dogs competing and the popularity of the breed in the area. The maximum in one show is five points.

As you can see, dog shows are purely competitive, like field trials and unlike obedience trials. People who become active in dog shows spend almost as much time and money at it as do those who become active in field trials.

Dog shows have been greatly criticized by many field trial people because they allow sporting dogs to become Champions without proving their ability in the field. Some of this criticism may be justified, but much of it is based on ignorance. The problem is that both activities are so demanding that not many people can become involved in both. Each person has to choose one or the other, so there is little understanding between the two. Both have contributed to the betterment of the retriever breeds, but each in its own way. If field trialers have kept and improved the working abilities of the breeds, then dog show people have kept and improved the dogs' soundness and appearance. Who, after all, wants a retriever that looks like a coyote?

Dog shows are conducted by local kennel clubs all over the country. They are under the control of the AKC, as are field trials (for retrievers at least) and obedience trials. The AKC can tell you where to find the club closest to you, if you would like to attend a dog show. I recommend that you do so, for you will not only see some very good physical specimens of your own breed, but you will also see many breeds that you have never even heard of, and you will get to talk to people whose interest in dogs is as intense as your own, but totally different in orientation.

The Future of Retrievers

Right now two retriever breeds are going through a very bad period. Both the Labrador and the golden are suffering from one of the worst misfortunes that can beset a breed—popularity! They have both been among the ten most popular breeds for several years, and no breed has ever gone through that kind of "success" and not been hurt. The other retriever breeds are more fortunate.

Chesapeakes are not often seen anywhere but at field trials and in duck blinds, and the other recognized retriever breeds are really rare anywhere in this country. When, for example, did you last see a flat-coated or curly-coated retriever or an Irish water spaniel?

Popularity brings about indiscriminate breeding by people who have no interest in the breed other than peddling a bunch of poorly bred pups for high prices, an activity that is usually possible when a breed starts through the popularity cycle. These people buy a cheap, worthless bitch, breed her to the nearest stud without any study of the pedigrees, and hang a high price on the pups. It has worked with many different breeds over the years. Of course, after a while the breed deteriorates to the point where it is difficult to sell good pups at reasonable prices. Then the serious breeders set about rebuilding the breed.

While popularity is the biggest problem in retrievers today, it is not the only one. Among the dogs produced by serious breeders, a duality has appeared in some of the sporting breeds that is not healthy. Some people breed for bench competition exclusively while others breed strictly for the field. This can lead to a total split in the breed, with two almost unrelated breeds emerging. This has happened to the pointer and setter to the extent that field dogs are registered with the Field Dog Stud Book while bench dogs are registered with the American Kennel Club. Granted, the AKC sponsors field trials for AKC-registered pointers and setters, but the really big pointer and setter trials are sponsored by the FDSB. For all practical purposes, the AKC pointer is a separate breed from the FDSB pointer. The same is true of the setter.

Even within breeds totally within one registry (AKC) there is an apparent growing split into "field type" and "bench type." The springer spaniel, for instance, suffers from this problem quite noticeably. Unfortunately, so do the Labrador and the golden retriever.

The problem underlying this duality is the competitiveness of both field trials and dog shows. It is so difficult to breed a dog that can win in field trials, for example, that it is hard for breeders to retain the basic conformation in their breeding programs and still remain competitive in the field. The same is true for bench dogs. In other words, the very competitiveness that is improving the breed in each specific area is at the same time causing a split between those areas.

This same competitiveness has made it extremely difficult for any one breeder to participate in both field and bench competition: there just isn't time and money enough to do both. Serious field trial competition requires total dedication; so does serious bench competition. No one can do both seriously. True, there are a few dual champions here and there, but not very many, not nearly enough to ensure the existence of a single type in their breed.

Those are the major problems facing retrievers today—too much popularity, and a potential split between field and bench types. Granted, both are now more of a problem to the Labrador and the golden than to the other retriever breeds, but who can say that this will not change? It takes so little to start a wave of popularity for a breed—a movie like *Rin-Tin-Tin* or *Lassie,* the endorsement of one major celebrity, a few television commercials featuring the breed. What the Lab and the golden are working their way through today could hit the other retriever breeds tomorrow.

The only cures for too much popularity are time and the continued dedication of serious breeders. Popularity will pass, given enough time. Many of those who have jumped on the Lab or golden bandwagon will leave it when the next breed craze hits. Then the serious breeders, both field and bench, who have been breeding good stock through this period of dangerously high popularity, will stabilize the quality of the breeds again. Other breeds have survived it; so will the retrievers.

As for the split in type, signs of improvement are already apparent.

The national breed clubs have taken a big step toward the solution of this problem by sponsoring the working certificate tests. With these, bench breeders can prove their stock in the field without getting into the licensed trial rat race. Unfortunately, the working certificate requirements do not include a blind retrieve, but they are being improved slowly, and the day will come when they will command a high level of respect even among field trialers.

It is also unfortunate that no comparable way exists for field breeders to prove the conformation quality of their breeding stock. The national breed clubs should develop a noncompetitive conformation test for field dogs that would approximate the working certificate tests for bench dogs. A dog with a basic conformation certificate and a good field trial record would be an excellent dog for breeding purposes. In fact, a dog with both a working certificate and a conformation certificate would be a good breeding prospect even if he had never competed in either a field trial or a dog show.

There is a growing interest in noncompetitive trials in all of the sporting breeds. Many national breed clubs, other than those for retrievers, offer working certificate tests. The Weimaraner

Club of America, for example, has a series of rating trials that offer an excellent way to prove the dog's ability to work in the uplands and in the duck blind. In fact, the Weimaraner Club rating trials for retrieving require a blind retrieve, which is not yet true for the working certificate tests for any of the retriever national breed clubs.

An organization called the North American Versatile Hunting Dog Association (NAVHDA) sponsors some really demanding but non-competitive field trials for the continental pointing breeds—German shorthairs, German wirehairs, weimaraners, vizslas, and so forth. Any dog that comes through the higher levels of these tests would be a whole lot of dog to hunt with, believe me.

Probably the ideal format for a trial would be something similar to that of the AKC obedience trial, in which a person can select any desirable level of competition, from none at all to fierce. If that format were available for both field and bench dogs, the problem of duality would be solved. Serious breeders could engage in both activities at an appropriate level instead of being forced by time and money limitations to concentrate on just one.

I do not advocate the elimination of competition from field trials and bench shows. Competition is good in that it has been the driving force behind the improvements we have made in the breeds over the past years. However, some choices should be available in the levels of competition required to prove the quality of breeding stock. The obedience trial format has a lot to offer in this area. If significant bench and field titles were available on a noncompetitive basis from the AKC, as they are in obedience, all breeders would have the opportunity to prove their dogs in both areas. The lack of a minimal title in each area would make it tough to sell puppies. Then, if there were competitive titles beyond these, the breeds would continue to improve, only there would be less of a split in type than there is now.

It is too bad that the obedience format was developed after the formats for field trials and dog shows. Had the reverse been true, these latter two might have offered noncompetitive titles, as does the truly effective obedience format. Whether such titles will ever be available remains to be seen. I hope they will.

INDEX